"*From Heartbreak to Wholeness* is a pure lighthouse, beaming its beautiful warming light through the thick fog of loss and suffering that each of us gets lost in at times. It's with breathtaking empathy, kindness, and knowing that Kristine Carlson signals the way back to the shore of ourselves, where we rediscover how to play and dance and rejoice in the sweet miracle of our lives, not despite loss but because of it."

—SARK, author and artist of *Succulent Wild Woman* and *Glad No Matter What*

"Kristine Carlson's brilliant new book, *From Heartbreak to Wholeness*, accomplishes two vital tasks—making sense of the pain we suffer in loss and giving us a luminous map to find our authentic joy again. A teacher of profound insight, she shows us how to turn life's moments of crisis into grist for the mill of awakening."

—Shauna L. Shapiro, Ph.D., author of *The Art and Science of Mindfulness*

"With compassion and love as only Kristine Carlson can do, this book takes you by the hand and helps you not only find your way back to life but walks with you on your hero's journey after loss."

—Christina Rasmussen, author of *Second Firsts*

"Kristine's work offers a pathway of deep healing for all those who have experienced loss. She writes from her heart and bases what she shares on her own direct experience. She has walked the path and has found her way to the other side, not by bypassing the canyon of heartbreak but by walking directly through it. I hope this book finds its way into the hands and hearts of those who need it most."

—Dustin DiPerna, author of *Streams of Wisdom*

"Kristine Carlson is the hero and speaks so eloquently about how to move through heartbreak and return to our natural state of joy. Her story will inspire you to frame your own journey in a way that will transform your perception of yourself. Kris shows you how to broadcast your happiness through having a love affair with your life!"

—Michelle Gielan, bestselling author of
Broadcasting Happiness

"Kristine Carlson is a luminous human being, one who is wise in matters of the heart. With her new book, *From Heartbreak to Wholeness,* she invites readers into a world that is so alive with feeling that it melts away the walls that pain and loss construct."

—Barnet Bain, filmmaker and author of
The Book of Doing and Being

From
Heartbreak
to Wholeness

Also by Kristine Carlson

Heartbroken Open: A Memoir Through Loss to Self-Discovery

Don't Sweat the Small Stuff for Moms

An Hour to Live, an Hour to Love

Don't Sweat the Small Stuff in Love

Don't Sweat the Small Stuff for Women

From
Heartbreak
to Wholeness

The Hero's Journey to Joy

Kristine Carlson

St. Martin's Press ☁ New York

www.stmartins.com

Designed by Steven Seighman

The Library of Congress Cataloging-in-Publication Data is available upon request.

ISBN 978-1-250-17043-9 (hardcover)
ISBN 978-1-250-18553-2 (ebook)

Our books may be purchased in bulk for promotional, educational, or business use. Please contact your local bookseller or the Macmillan Corporate and Premium Sales Department at 1-800-221-7945, extension 5442, or by email at MacmillanSpecialMarkets@macmillan.com.

First Edition: June 2018

10 9 8 7 6 5 4 3 2 1

155.537
C

For Lisa.
I'm so proud to be your best friend.
Thank you for choosing to be the hero.
You are my hero.

Contents

Acknowledgments

A book like this is born as a collaboration of many conversations and the support of many people over many years. But there are always a handful of people that stand out as being truly instrumental in the process of birthing a book. There are so many people to thank:

My parents, Pat and Ted Anderson, for raising me to be a strong woman with a deep belief in Christ and a benevolent God.

Richard, for always being present and loving me; I feel so held by your spirit.

My daughters, Jazz and Kenna, who are always my best cheerleaders and who make me want to be a hero every day. Devon, my son-in-law, who is the best police officer and father I know—I'm so proud of you.

My grandchildren, who bring me so much joy.

All of my closest devoted friends who have lovingly supported me all these healing years: Carole Foley-Stewart, Lisa Marino, Melanie Desautels, TJ Nelson, Laura Hulburd, Simin Kaabi, Jane Carone, Karen Salmansohn, Christine Arylo, Mary Vesey, Nancy Hughes (the best cousin ever), Marcy Cole, Nancy Katz, Diana Cole, Dana Dowell, Jen Rode, Sharon Piserchio, Karen Rhodes, Marni

Posl, Amy Ahlers, Alissa Brownrigg-Small, Julia Akunding, Liz Malone, and Renny Madlena.

KC Baker, for inspiring the leader in me and bringing my voice to the world. Robin Sharma, for your friendship and the conversation that inspired the depth in this book. Dorian Aiello, for exposing me to the Mankind Project. Celeste Fine, my agent, and her associate John Maas, for believing in me and finding the right publishing home for this book to be birthed. Alana Leigh, for all of your heart support and inspiring study and conversation of ego. Jennifer Loftus, for being a new friend and supporter. Kim Serafini, for all of our laughter and exposing me to a new conversation of neuroscience. Christina Rasmussen, for your great work and being my soul sister while we walk this parallel journey together. Shauna Shapiro, for your eyes on the early chapters and for breaking my fall so my foot was my only injury. Mike Robbins, for always remembering Richard and speaking about him. Alexandra Franzen, for your encouragement and support and for a lovely retreat in Hawaii. Rich Dutra-St. John and Yvonne St. John-Dutra, for being the heroes you are and helping me remember why I came to this earth. You are the transformational leaders I have learned so much from over the years, and you have been my best friends. Rosa Aguayo, for allowing this book to work on you and validate the journey of healing in these pages as you drove me everywhere with my broken right foot. Justin Hilton, for introducing me to Debra. Michael Flamini at St. Martin's Press, a wonderful editor, who felt this book from the beginning. And finally, the biggest thanks of all, to Debra Evans. She has been the greatest gift to me in this birthing process—she inspired me to bring my best self forward. Debra is a master; her expertise as an editor brought ease and grace to this process. A true book doula she is! Thank you, Debra, for being the hero you are!

Introduction

Your task is not to seek for love, but merely to seek and find all the barriers within yourself that you have built against it.

—RUMI

All around the world people are suffering due to heartbreak of some kind. Some have lost a partner or friend through a breakup, divorce, or death. There are those who are alienated from family members due to conflict or irreconcilable differences. For others, there is the painful loss of purpose that can happen when a job ends or the nest empties. There can be devastation in losing one's home due to financial crisis or natural disaster. When a person goes through an illness, there can be the loss of the way life was before the diagnosis shattered their safety and their identity as a healthy person. Whatever the form, loss leaves us heartbroken, vulnerable, raw, and in fear of the unknown.

This book is not only for people who have gone through loss; it is for those of you who have gone through anything. It will address loss, but more than that, it will teach you how to recover to live your most vibrant life. In the coming pages, you will read about my story of loss, so there is no need for me to go into it here. I speak to you, heart to heart; one broken heart mended, to whatever form your heart may be in now, which is likely feeling in pieces.

We often think of loss as being the *big* losses, but truth is, we experience heartache all the time, although we don't always acknowledge smaller disappointments and curveballs as those things we may be grieving. At times, we may call it anxiety and depression. But what if it's not anxiety or depression? What if what we are really going through is grief? Anxiety and depression do, of course, happen independent of grief, but for many of us, what we're feeling may be the malaise of unacknowledged loss piled upon loss. What if we really don't understand the opportunity that is present to us in loss? The Western world has traditionally been wildly ill equipped to do grief and understand how to heal. At a certain point in my own loss, I realized that grief was the great housecleaner; this one great loss brought enough reason for grief to clean out all the pipes that contained the layers of loss that had built up throughout my lifetime. *Whoosh!* All those tears for all those years!

Sometimes the healing is quick, and sometimes it takes weeks, months, or years. Any great loss will lead you to the gateway of transformation, and no matter why you're in loss, transformation is messy, just as birthing a child is messy. A miracle happens on the other side of that birthing process, but it's certainly not pretty going through labor and delivery. This process of change can look and feel insane from the outside looking in because you don't feel at all like yourself—and you don't act like yourself, either. I'll tell you now . . . you're not yourself. You're literally changing form in this process of healing. In fact, due to this loss, you'll never be the same again. You aren't the same for having loved and lived, and you won't be the same as you walk through the doorway of awakening that loss provides.

Here's the good news: As you move forward in crisis and through the stages of healing presented in these pages, you'll evolve into someone better and more capable of giving and receiving greater love. In time, you'll feel at home in your body again and more authentic to your true nature than you ever have before. You'll feel more alive, and you'll access even more joy than you thought possible.

This book is not about how to grieve your losses as much as it is about how to transform your heartbreak into rich, authentic expression and allow it to catalyze you into wholeness. Although I address the importance of grief in the early chapters, this is a book designed to let you choose to be the hero of your story, and it's going to teach you how to frame your story in a way that reveals who you are.

HOW TO USE THIS BOOK

Grief is tough stuff. It puts you through the contractions of labor that open you, as you empty out your emotions and let go of your attachments, to birthing a new life. That is why this book contains nine chapters, symbolic of the nine months of gestation from the fluttering of a new life to its birth into the world. Your process of healing your heartbreak and returning to wholeness and happiness is its own process of incubation and evolution. No one can tell you how much time it will take to heal.

In telling my own story of healing and those of others, and guiding you through yours, I have chosen to use the "hero's journey," as it is an archetypal story that belongs to all of us. Joseph Campbell is most noted for bringing this ancient wisdom to modern times. It's the collectively inherited story of human unfolding, woven together from world mythologies throughout time, and it serves as a profound map. It helps us to see that we are on a path of meaning and purpose even when fear and grief leave us confused and grappling. It offers us guideposts even when the way home appears to be wholly lost.

As I witnessed my own healing path, I realized I had walked the hero's journey. It's important to note, though, that my use of the hero's journey is not in any way a depiction of Joseph Campbell's extraordinary mythological work. It is my own interpretation of how the hero's journey applies to the process of healing loss and grief, moving through the stages of recovery, and returning to wholeness and joy. An equally important body of work is that of Maureen Murdock, the author of *The Heroine's Journey*. Murdock's brilliant analysis of a woman's search for wholeness and meaning has been a source of wisdom that I have applied at pivotal times in my life. However, I have chosen here to refer primarily to the *hero's* journey as the more gender-neutral term because this book is written for both men and women. On a personal level, while I've always walked the heroine's journey, healing my own heartbreak (as you will read in the pages to come) has involved reclaiming my masculine qualities in the process of becoming a fully integrated woman. There came a point where I consciously chose not to be a victim of my circumstances but instead to walk the hero's journey toward my new life.

At the end of each chapter, you will find exercises and processes that I've created to both deepen and accelerate your healing journey. This process section will help you solidify your insights and integrate what you learn. The whole basis for processing is to find the meaning of what's happened. It's so important for us to put all events in order for ourselves so that we're not living in victimhood and being assaulted over and over. We can move forward.

At the end of each chapter, I will first lead you through a specific Soul Mantra designed to relax you into a state of openness and affirmation. Then I lead you through a Soul Inquiry section, a series of journaling questions that invoke your honest responses to inspire a transformational writing process that will assist you in framing your story. After you have explored these questions, you will come to the concluding section of the chapter titled Your New Story. There is writing space provided where you can get to the essence of the lessons you're learning about yourself and the story you may be see-ing in new ways. Please keep in mind that you don't have to be a writer to do these exercises; you just need to respond to the question in or-der to receive your own inner wisdom. This is an internal process for you to discover the hero within you. In short, I want you to use the processes at the end of each chapter to shift and change and become the hero of your own epic journey as you frame your story; of course, I'll show you how.

Seeing yourself as the hero may feel foreign at first, a little un-comfortable if you feel that you've been at the mercy of life, battered by adverse circumstances. My hope is that you see your own courage in the coming pages and are empowered to choose differently, that you get unstuck, and that you feel my guidance and encouragement along the way. You're not alone. There are millions of other people walking alongside you for different reasons, all on the path to heal-ing from heartbreak.

My journey has been a wild ride—a roller coaster that has required me to ride it with my arms high above my head as I take the curves in surrender. I have had some challenging initiations and astound-ing spiritual experiences, shared here, that are out of this world, some-times defying logic and reason. While I don't know why some have extraordinary spiritual experiences and others don't seem to, my hope in sharing some of mine with you here is that they will open you to or remind you of the grace, help, and divine love that surround us always, especially in those moments when we can't see the light.

YOUR STORY IS YOUR MEDICINE

The richness of "story" becomes the focus here because it is ultimately the stories we tell ourselves within the quiet of our own minds that have the biggest impact on our daily lives and shaping our destinies. That's why it becomes so relevant for you to frame your story through the hero's lens. Also, there is such power in sharing your story of lessons learned; we have always learned, from the time we were children, through story. When you walk the path of the hero, you empower others to do the same by your example.

I have met so many leaders along this path of story-sharing who have walked the hero's path. These people have suffered greatly and transformed their loss into greater meaning—and it is the power of their story and how they each chose to be the hero that has helped them become greater leaders. In the face of adversity and loss, we all fall down, but it's how you get up and stand and step forward that reveals who you are. Years ago, in my living room after I had written a memoir, *Heartbroken Open: A Memoir Through Loss to Self-Discovery*, I would hold Heartbroken Open circles for women. As we moved around the circle, the healing salve became evident in each woman's voice as she shared her story of loss. The power to heal comes in sharing our story.

THE JOURNEY FROM HEARTBREAK TO JOY

At the heart of my message to you is this: You have one choice in how you move through the stages of healing presented in these pages. Are you a victim, or are you a hero? I have always seen that there are two possible paths, and you are likely standing at the fork in the road right now. There's only one way to go if you deeply desire to live and return to an empowered life of joy. You must follow the mindset and path of the hero, and I will show you how to do that early in the book. Through stories and examples, I will teach you how to turn your story into the hero's journey, and I will show you how you can look at the circumstances you face right now in a way that will empower you to live with greater meaning and renewed purpose despite what you've been through.

My promise to you is that you will feel hopeful as you read this book. You will feel guided and know that I'm holding your hand through each page. I'm with you. We are connected heart to heart. Even though I don't know the details of your unique story, I understand what you've been through. And I want you to know: You are not just going to survive—you are going to do *so* much more than that. You are going to grow and evolve in ways that will change the way you show up in the world. You are going to blossom in ways that will show *you* who you are. My loss did that for me. It awakened me and showed me who I am. And I'm no different than you—except, maybe, that I had so many tools from having lived a happy life and practicing the philosophy that was born from my beloved late husband Richard Carlson's work in the *Don't Sweat the Small Stuff* books. I'm giving all of that to you here in these pages.

While you likely came to this book thinking it is about loss, what you will discover is that this book will teach you more about how to live from this point forward. You will transform. You will heal. You will emerge greater than you can possibly imagine. You will return to wholeness—a wholeness that has always existed within you. Moreover, you will return to joy.

Treasure the gifts of life and love.

Chapter 1

Initiation by Crisis

The Promise of Chapter 1—Your life has changed. You have stepped into the unknown. The next choices you make will determine whether you are the victim or the hero of your own precious life story. Take my hand. I will help you to choose wisely.

My journey began when an ordinary day in early December—one that included morning dishes, getting the kids off to school, running errands, completing end-of-year school projects with my daughters (both in high school), and simply doing what I always did while preparing for the holidays—was shattered by a single phone call. Like a milk carton, the doctor told me the love of my life had "expired." A silent killer in the form of a pulmonary embolism made its way from his leg to explode in his lung, taking my husband's life without warning on the descent of a flight into New York . . . that day that turned our lives upside down and devastated our family.

Richard and I met in college and shared a fairy-tale romance for twenty-five years. We became a family of four as we raised two amazing daughters. Our cup ran over with a marriage made of deep cherishing, devotion, nurturing communication, vital inspiration, and unending gratitude for each other. We were mostly pals, with a true understanding of what our partnership meant. No matter what was happening in our lives, we were able to meet each other with a kind of respect that evolved over the years into greater reverence. To us, there was no one that stood on higher ground or who was more able to offer comfort, encouragement, and support. It didn't matter if we were miles apart in our travels for business or play; with few exceptions, we started our days with "good morning, honey" by phone or enjoying coffee in the early morning hours, sharing our hopes and dreams, working on chapters of a book together, and strategizing about parenting our kids. One of the keys to the success of our marriage was our listening; we really listened to each other—especially to the feelings behind the words, leading to a deeper understanding where we connected from heart to heart. He wanted to know what mattered to me, and I loved the ongoing discovery of what he felt passionate about. When Richard died unexpectedly at the age of forty-five, I had no idea how I would continue to breathe, much less move forward in life without his physical presence.

Most of my adult life, I lived under the grand illusion that Richard and I had control over our destiny. We were kind people doing good work in the world and were devoted to our family, friends, and global community. As long as we worked hard, stayed in our integrity, and remained in love, everything would go according to our well-laid plans. My role as a wife and mom was to hold space for everyone like a crystal in a clock so they would have what they needed. I was holding all I had dreamed of as a young girl, the perfect life.

Yes, we had the ideal life, but truth is, I wasn't fully grateful for it. I had been lulled into the kind of complacency that often comes from success. I was sleepwalking through my life, and I didn't even know it. My kids were growing up; I had been feeling inklings of something that was incomplete, and deep questions nagged at me daily: *What is my life's purpose and passion beyond being a good wife and mother? What else do I have to contribute, and how can I serve and honor my life here?*

Even though I had coauthored *Don't Sweat the Small Stuff in Love* and written *Don't Sweat the Small Stuff for Women*, both *New York Times* bestsellers, I hadn't owned my career as an author. I'll never regret giving all that I did to Richard as his partner so that he could fulfill his life's work and leave his legacy; nor will I ever regret my devotion to nurturing our daughters—they are my most precious gifts, and it is a privilege to be their mother. Family means everything to me. I love Richard and miss him every day. I can hear his voice and laughter imprinted on my soul; I close my eyes, and there he is with his exaggerated cleft chin and twinkling ocean-blues smiling back at me. The pain of his loss was indescribably intense, and it lasts to this day. Nothing about this experience has been easy.

Yet that unimaginable phone call didn't halt my life. I can now see that the loss of my partner was my initiation—the divine event that changed my life so suddenly that it led me to the gateway of transformation, just as yours has and will, too. It led me to the answers to the questions I didn't even know I had been asking. After the numbness of shock subsided, my husband's death breathed new life into me, and I was awake and *feeling* everything.

Why did this happen? Why did my heart open from this loss?

When you are standing at a fork in the road brought on by heartbreak—whether that heartbreak is caused by a death, a divorce, a breakup, a diagnosis, news of some kind that has shattered life as you know it, or any other kind of soul-shaking loss—there are only two possible paths to choose from. Which path you choose boils down to one question:

Are you going to be a victim, or are you going to be a hero?

You can choose to be a victim, or you can choose to be a hero. Here's what both look like: The victim, head down, slumped and broken, wallows in self-pity at the fork in the road, unable to get up. The hero feels just as broken but stands up, shakes off the self-pity, and moves forward, stepping, albeit slowly, into the journey ahead.

I am here to tell you that there is only one choice to make every day, and that is to be open to this experience and what it will reveal. While you may have a difficult time as you lever back and forth between these choices, ultimately you must choose to be a hero. You must ask yourself, *What would a hero do in this situation?* (If you don't know what the hero would do, that's OK, too. Please continue reading.) Even if you do not like the cards you've been dealt, you must play the hand and say, "I will be the hero who meets the challenge of this loss and allows it to do its work on me. I will meet this demand, this call from my soul to live. I will be a hero who overcomes obstacles, leans into my fears, annihilates my unhealthy ego, and learns and grows from these circumstances. I will find my way as a hero and do the inner work necessary to emerge as a whole and complete victor. I will awaken."

Making the conscious choice to see yourself as a hero and the victor over the adversity you face is one of the most important decisions of your life. As the journey of healing unfolds throughout the pages of this book, the reasons for this will be increasingly clear.

THE INITIATION—INTO THE UNKNOWN

In the hero's journey, laid out in the arc by Joseph Campbell, the initiation is a crisis event that shatters all the illusions of your life. It completely changes your direction, and you don't know where it is you are going. You are standing at the precipice of the unknown. You might as well be standing on the edge of the Grand Canyon wondering how you will ever get to the other side. All you know is that life looks very different now, and there is confusion; it feels like you are in a foreign country without a language you understand. This initiation may have obliterated your beliefs about what love is and what you need in your life to make it complete. It brings you to your knees with shards of glass around your feet. Your old ways of going about your life are no longer sufficient.

And how could it be otherwise? In my very bones, I understand how you may be feeling. Your heart is completely broken and your dreams no more. You have a deep knowing that your life is never going to be the same. There is nothing in your being that isn't screaming, "My life has changed!" With your whole life tipped upside down, you feel numb from the shock and in total disbelief; heavy-hearted and full of dread, you sense a long and desolate journey ahead of you. I know—I felt it, too. It's very likely that you feel disconnected from everyone around you, even the people you're the closest to, because they can't possibly understand what you are going through. It feels odd, as if you are looking through a new lens that makes everything on the outside appear "normal," but feeling like scrambled eggs on the inside. You feel as though you are in one of those snow globes encased in glass and looking out. Their lives keep going on; yours has been rendered unrecognizable to you. While going through the motions into the unknown, you feel overwhelmed with anxiety and fear. Be gentle with yourself, my dear, understanding that you are vulnerable right now because you're going through unprecedented change and moving into an inner world of uncharted territory. I know it's scary.

This event is, in fact, the entry point into transformation. It changes the trajectory of your life; it is the commencement of your journey. As awful as it feels, it is really your heart being broken open. You may not know it yet, but this is actually the gateway to a new life; you are birthing a new life as you birth your story in these upcoming pages. Yes, you have entered into the unknown, into the mystery, where life is not going to be the same, and you may be kicking and screaming all the way. Where hope comes in is that you're going to discover and uncover the ideas and beliefs upon which the illusion that is now shattered was built. Up until now, you didn't know that life could be different. You're asking, *Who am I now—who am I without this love (without this family, this job, this sense of security, this self-image, this identity)?*

As you are standing on unstable ground with your identity in question, it doesn't help matters that you feel like your friends and family are now relating to you differently, too. You may already have noticed that people's default reaction to your struggle will be to treat you as a victim. Everyone you encounter, whether new connections you've met through your crisis, friends and family members who have been at your side for the whole journey, or strangers who are hearing about your experience for the first time, will act as though you are damaged . . . as though you are someone to whom something has "happened." They are filled with sympathy and want to treat you with kid gloves. They don't really know what to say, so they err on the side of deference as they repeat phrases of condolence that feel trite to the grief-stricken. Of course, this comes from a good place, and these people mean well. There is nothing wrong with that. But it means that so many external forces are treating you like a person to be pitied, and it's all too easy to let these voices dictate your truth throughout your journey, making it all the more important to see yourself in a different way so that you don't get lost in this mindset of survival. You are standing on such rich, fertile ground for your growth, and there's so much more to come.

DEVELOPING THE HERO'S MINDSET

I remember sitting at our fireplace in one of our well-worn leather chairs within days of that fateful phone call. I could see both paths before me: one where I would drown in self-pity and sorrow, and possibly a fifth of vodka, and one where I would honor my love, his life, and all of the blessings we had created together in our twenty-five years. I didn't know what the journey would hold, but I knew that I had to step into what was before me. I would honor Richard with my life. His life had changed mine, and we were so blessed. My heart knew that this was my soul work—my time for change and my time to grow. My time to awaken. While of course I had those days when it was difficult not to pull the covers up and stay in bed, I would remind myself that doing so represented death to me. I had to live. My thoughts whispered to me to rise amidst the ashes of my old life as I hesitantly embraced and tiptoed into my new one.

As you step over the threshold into a new and unknown world, you very quickly have to choose: *Will I be the hero of my own life, right here in the middle of this situation that I do not want?* Randy Pausch gave us a great example in his book *The Last Lecture.* After he found out that he had cancer, he felt he had not honored his life's purpose up to that point. He went into his classroom and talked about leaving a legacy before you die, and this Last Lecture would go viral on the internet. He did indeed play the cards that he was dealt, and he left this world as a hero of his journey.

If you haven't done this early in your crisis, or you are now realizing that you may be the victim of your story, you can choose to be the hero from this point forward. It's never too late to discover a new and healthier way to live and to be in your life. You are in charge of how you navigate this path. The heart may still be broken as you choose to stand in your own journey, acknowledging how difficult it may be but committing to yourself that you will move forward. When Richard died, I chose right away. But you can choose to be the hero at any time. I have a friend, Carolyn Moor, who was out on a date with her husband on Valentine's Day years ago, and there was an accident. She lived and he died. Suddenly a young widow in her midthirties, raising two young daughters and continuing her career as a designer, Carolyn lived many years in a fog, victimized by what had happened. No one is prepared for sudden loss. The rug is pulled out from under your feet. Years later, she was mentored by Rabbi Shmuley Boteach on the TLC television series *Shalom in the Home*. With his support and inspiration, she broke free of that fog and chose to step in and be the hero. Now, she is a leader among widows with her extremely successful online community, the Modern Widows Club. I share her story to show you that you can choose differently at any time and have the same thriving result.

At whatever juncture the decision is made, the hero is one who chooses not to be the victim of the circumstances at hand. The mind will fight you in choosing to be the hero. Like sticky tape, the ego will latch on to the thoughts of self-pity and the reasons why you should crawl into a hole. The mind will struggle back and forth between these two mindsets. But the hero understands that this event—this loss, this tragedy, this incomprehensible change—is part of the life curriculum. Life itself is a classroom, and you have just entered your graduate school coursework in heart mending and management, a course where you will learn how your suffering serves you and one that will be carefully designed for your soul growth. The hero acknowledges the pain and the anger and sees it all and feels it intensely. But the hero is not going to indulge in too much pity or tarry too long in past regret. It doesn't mean that feelings are suppressed, but there's no long rest in self-pity. Self-pity will suck you under, and you won't come out feeling empowered and ready for the journey. The hero must live life and function despite a broken heart. Life continues on no matter what. It doesn't work any other way. If you were diagnosed with cancer, you wouldn't just stop. You would ask, *How do I* live *with this illness, this disease? What is my plan for getting healthy? How will I fight this?* You will do what needs to be done; you will play the hand that you've been dealt.

Of course, it's OK to acknowledge that this crisis, this pain, is *not* what you want. *This is what has been given me. I don't like it, but I'm going to deal with it.* Drop into what's real for you, but don't stay in the trenches of pity. Pity can become a self-loathing act that sabotages all efforts to step into being the hero and keeps you from stepping into the journey of healing.

When you choose at the fork in the road to be the hero, this is where you get to have your power. You don't get to choose who dies or who leaves you, or what happens to you, but you get to choose how you stand and how you move forward. You get to choose how you think and where you put your attention and focus.

At the precipice of what may feel like a personal event horizon, examining your beliefs and perception is mission critical. The circumstances you are facing won't make or break you, but they do reveal who you are. What are the thoughts that you repeat over and over again that come from your past? How do you latch onto those tapes that play over and over in your head, those attempts at renegotiating the events of the past—trying to undo the unthinkable, unimaginable event that has rocked your world? How do you talk to yourself in the quiet of your own inner world? What kind of feelings do your thoughts give rise to? The alliance of your thoughts, words, ideas, and feelings determines the lens through which you view the world. Your beliefs—those thoughts that you have repeated as truths over and over thousands of times (in turn, life-affirming and limiting)—make up the agreement you have made with reality and how you view these circumstances. And whatever your agreement is will determine whether you are a victim or a hero.

Sometimes we aren't aware of the agreement we've made with reality—the one that dictates, as Einstein said, whether we live in a friendly or unfriendly universe—until it's in our face. In my What Now? online mentorship program, uncovering and understanding this invisible pact you have with yourself is a life-changing realization and a huge pivot toward becoming the hero. We look at the teeter-totter upon which you sit at this critical moment. Your agreement is made from all of your habits, and you are in the habit, generally, of being the victim or victor in most situations. Where is your agreement with reality going to take you? Wherever you are, you can shift the balance to the side you wish to be on. Your circumstances are on one seat while you sit on the other side. Which side will carry the weight? You get to choose.

CHOOSING TO SURRENDER— THE BEAUTIFUL PARADOX

Ironically, the first step toward healing on the hero's path requires surrender. It is in the choice to allow for healing that you will find your power to step in. You are in the situation where you find your-self because of circumstances that were beyond your control, even though there are times you may blame yourself and feel guilt for what has happened. Whether you are going through the loss of a loved one, the undoing of a relationship, or the loss of your health or a job, much—if not all—is far from what you would choose. That's why it's so important to take back choice.

People will tell you all sorts of things about the grieving process. They will tell you that it's a series of steps that everyone passes through in much the same sequence. Most people think of the loss of love through the lens of the five stages of the classic Kübler-Ross model: denial, anger, bargaining, depression, and acceptance. I have been through this process myself, and I work with people going through loss all the time. These five stages are a helpful rubric, and certainly have pioneered a path to give people permission to grieve, but they do not capture the universal reality. What's missing from this model is the idea that our path is a journey whose transformation depends on the choices we make along the way. Harvard researcher Shawn Achor, author of *The Happiness Advantage,* has said, "What we've been finding is that scientifically, happiness could actually be a choice even when life is difficult." If happiness is a choice, then how we navigate this time of initiation is also a choice.

I had lived under the illusion that I had control over my life, but my heartbreak wasn't something I could fight or control. I had to open and receive, and that would first require me to *surrender.* I had to re-ceive from my family, my friends, my community. I learned that one of the most profound choices I could make was wholly invisible—it was to surrender to the unknown, to the mystery. It's in surrender that you receive. Grace and love are present in that opening, in that heartbreak, and you call on them as you accept that you are broken open but you are awake. You aren't likely feeling all that empowered yet. You are like a wild animal at this point, feeling wounded and wishing to retreat to solitude and isolation. What I learned in the wild is that I have control only over the choices I make every day, beginning with putting my feet on the ground every morning. This is far from limiting; it is truly empowering. It all happens in baby steps—one right after the next.

I will show you how to tap into the power of choices for shaping and guiding your journey from loss to joy. Our choices give us an opportunity to connect more deeply and to listen to divine guidance, allowing our hearts to open to our internal wisdom. As we are helped and supported by friends, family, and community, they show us the way to take care of the practical things that need to be done, and ultimately allow us to grieve and live on our own terms. Choices are the key to taking a bit of power back and stepping forward from the trenches of grief and into a new life that embraces loss and its transformation.

With each step we take as we move through these stages of our healing, we have the power to influence how and when we get back to wholeness. It all starts with the choice we make at the time of initiation to be a hero. Your journey will be made up of thousands of choices along the way, and I will give you guidance for how to make these choices throughout, as you move along this soul path. But no choice is more important than this initial choice of not being the victim of your story.

As we discussed in the Introduction, with this first chapter you are beginning a deep call-and-response process with yourself that will be facilitated by the **Soul Mantra** affirmation and two journaling sections: **The Soul Inquiry** and **Your New Story**. I'll prompt you with questions designed to help you reach within, and I encourage you to bring kindness, curiosity, and courage to the way you listen to yourself. The quality of your listening and the honesty that you allow to come forth from your heart can be miraculous in their ability to break open the possibilities of a new future—a future where your heart is healed, your mind is inspired, and you're in love with the life you are living. And if that seems like an impossible dream right now, I only ask you to keep reading, keep journaling, and decide to trust the process and let it unfold. I'm with you every step of the way.

> **SOUL MANTRA:**
>
> Close your eyes. Breathe deeply into your belly.
> Repeat for five to ten minutes:
>
> *I am open to all that is. It is as it is.*

....

THE SOUL INQUIRY:
COMMENCING THE JOURNEY

Journal uncensored and answer these questions. As you do so, you are writing your own story and beginning the journey home into wholeness. Your answers will reveal what you need to know in this stage of healing. Here are the questions for the commencement of your journey:

1. What was your crisis event—your initiation?
2. What was ordinary life to you before your heartbreak happened? How is your life now?
3. How have your plans for your life changed since your crisis event?
4. Have you noticed particular thought patterns—those "tapes" that can play on repeat in your mind? What are those tapes, and how do they make you feel?
5. What illusions have you been living under about love and life? How has having these illusions pierced broken you open?
6. What do you need to understand to develop the hero's mindset?

....

Your New Story • *transformational writing process*

You stand at a brand-new and very powerful moment of choice.
How are your current choices impacting your life? Are you ready
to choose to be the hero? When you are ready, write about how
life has shattered for you and if you are ready to make a commitment
to choose the hero's path, starting from wherever you are right
now.

_____

_____

_____

_____

_____

_____

_____

_____

_____

_____

_____

_____

_____

_____

_____

_____

_____

_____

Please visit

FROMHEARTBREAKTOWHOLENESS.COM

to retrieve your soul mantra meditation downloads.

Chapter 2

Preparing for the Journey

The Promise of Chapter 2—You are preparing for a journey of healing and are now "packing" for the inner expedition. What do you need in order to go through this healing process? Your needs are singularly important at this moment, and I will help you to clarify what they are. Read on. Page by page, you will feel empowered by your choices and soothed by the supreme self-care you give yourself.

You have been led to the threshold of profound change, initiated into what at times feels like an exclusive club whose members are holders of the secret knowledge of what it feels like to live with a heart that still beats even though it is pained and broken. It seems impossible, yet there it is—thump, thump, thump, thump. The course of your life has changed; a new and winding road stretches out before you, but you don't know where you're going or what it will look like when you get there. What you do know is that it's all very disorienting. Initiation feels like you've been cut off from all that you know, much of which was a life you loved. With Richard's death, I felt like God had had an Alzheimer's moment. "What?!" I cried. "Aren't you fifty years off?!" The future that I had imagined was gone in an instant, and it was the beginning of a pilgrimage that I have since come to understand—and one that I am here to help you navigate so that it is far less daunting.

It is no ordinary journey you're getting ready to embark upon. It's a retrieval of the aspects of yourself that have gone missing in the wake of the event that has altered the fabric of your life, and there are important steps to the mending process. You wouldn't send military heroes to war if they weren't in prime shape, or without the gear they would need for a safe passage, and it's no exaggeration to say that your journey is a matter of equal importance for which you need to feel adequately emotionally equipped. This is where you put your stake in the ground for your happiness and wholeness, and all of that matters to your future dreams—those you cannot even begin to imagine yet. There's no quitting. You are the survivor. Now is the time to prepare to move forward so that you will not only survive but will eventually thrive. This is your first step toward wholeness, and you want to be prepared.

Those first days, weeks, and months of the unimaginable, life is complex. No matter how a relationship ends or other devastating loss occurs, it leaves the gap of separation, a missing piece in your puzzle, and that means making adjustments for changing and healing as life continues on to fill that hole. The pain of grief and the fear of being alone are at times unbearable. In this early part of the journey, the victim surrenders to fear, but the hero surrenders mind, body, and soul to lean in, facing fear and finding the meaning and soul growth in what has happened.

An important part of beginning your journey is finding the "message in the mess"—the revelation to which your loss is pointing. It was actually Oprah who helped me see mine, one year after Richard's death. In front of 20 million viewers, Oprah placed her hand on top of mine as she asked me a question: "Kris, do you think Richard's death has given you the gift of feeling your life?" With tears the size of golf balls and a knot in my throat, I could only nod my head and barely audibly croak out "Yes" to this question that pierced me with clarity. **The gift of feeling my life** was the message in the mess. Understanding and embracing this message not only gave me the fuel I needed to move forward but also changed my life as it transformed my circumstances into a life lesson to be learned and a message to be shared. My intention is that you, too, gain this clarity while traveling through these pages with me, if it hasn't already come to you.

The journey you're preparing for is the journey of your own healing and its unique form and flow. Your grief will inform you. Your body will show you how, alternately whispering and shouting for your attention through its painful reminders. Your tummy may hurt, and you will need to cry more. You may cough to get the grief moving. You may feel fatigued and anxious. All of these ways your body is screaming: **Feel it to heal it and express it out!**

Heartbreak of some kind is the red pushpin on the map of where you find yourself right now, and articulating what has been lost is part of what will mend you. Each of us takes a turn on the carousel of comings and goings. Beloveds die; marriages and long-term relationships end; friendships fall apart. In a divorce or breakup, there is that particularly searing pain to be reconciled—that we often go into a surreal no-contact space, knowing that someone we have intimately shared our lives with is now off-limits . . . here but not here. Sometimes it's getting older that breaks our hearts, when the way we have known ourselves disappears. And sometimes heartbreak happens when we receive the news that our health has changed. Heartbreak happens in an identity crisis and can come and go many times in our lives.

While I was in a meeting one day, my phone whistled at me, and I flipped it over to see a text message from one of my closest friends.

> I'm in the doctor's office—getting dressed and waiting for him to come in. I had my mammogram. They are telling me I have cancer. Kris, I can't believe this. I have breast cancer.

With a chill running up my spine, I excused myself from the boardroom, and without hesitation I rang her. This was not a text conversation. "Are you certain that's what they said?" In a hushed tone that was slow and deliberate, Lisa replayed the events of the previous days. In a state of shock and disbelief, she told me she had felt a lump in her right breast, and when visiting the doctor with her mother, who was being treated for breast cancer, Lisa mentioned it to him. He examined her on the spot and sent her right upstairs for a mammogram. "Yes, it's true. I've got it. Wow. I never thought I would get breast cancer." Who does? One out of five women will. That spring I had three friends who were called back for a recheck. So was I. But Lisa was the *one*.

The weeks that followed included all of the disbelief and shock that is a normal response to life-changing news. Suddenly, Lisa's world was tipped upside down, and when the shock and fog of disbelief cleared, she had a new focus. It was about her health and establishing what changes needed to take place. She researched diet and cancer treatments and spoke to energy healers and specialists. Her world had changed, and it became about how she would shift her body into a healthy gear that would live with and survive cancer. Her world had shattered, and she knew this was her time to awaken. Things had to change—she had to change—and the stakes were high. She had stage 3 breast cancer. It was aggressive and had already made it to her bloodstream.

Lisa is a natural-born giver and caretaker. She has always put everyone else first, never acknowledging her own needs over another's. This time in her life was going to be different; it was going to be about Lisa taking care of Lisa in the same way she had taken care of everyone around her. Immediately she not only began to make changes in her physical world but also began taking a deep dive into her emotional world, asking herself the bravest questions: *How did I allow cancer to grow in my body, and what fear, anger, and resentment are present that need to shift in order for me to be free?*

As her best friend, my intention was for her to know she could have 100 percent access to me. We discussed everything openly. She immediately decided to have a double mastectomy, and I was there supporting her and her husband as she did so.

The days before her surgery, we meditated and prayed together. She was stoic and strong, but I wasn't surprised when she finally realized that the next day she would say good-bye to her breasts forever—and there were fear and tears. We sat, arms wrapped around each other, mourning the breasts that had nursed four children and pleasured her sexually—knowing that she was commencing a journey that would require unthinkable courage from her and would demand that she change her thinking and her life. It would demand that she put herself before anyone else.

During her chemo treatments—her red devil moments—Lisa withdrew into the silence of her cocoon to heal. She didn't want to be around people. This was the first step she made in learning to care for herself first, her first empowered choice. There were those around her who wanted to make it about them; they wanted to be her companion and show up for her, but in their way, not her way. Her husband explained that they just wanted to show their love and said she shouldn't isolate herself. She should allow them in to help her.

In a heartfelt plea to me, she spoke with frustration, saying, "I don't want to feel obligated to smile or make someone else feel more comfortable as I'm going through this. I just don't have the energy to give right now in any kind of exchange of niceties or conversation." I completely understood and began to campaign on her behalf—helping her help herself. She began to realize that this was her first step of liberation from her old habits and past way of being. She immediately woke up to the idea that cancer had showed up to teach her a new way to live. This was her message in the mess, and she was completely aware of it in the beginning of what would be a hell-wrought year of healing. She would rid herself not only of cancer but of the ways she had lived that no longer served her. This was her gift of a new life.

This is the beauty of preparing for a journey of healing. It's the crystal clarity that happens as you let go of your old way of life and surrender to the new one—the one that will allow you to survive and eventually thrive beyond anything that you can imagine at this stage of healing.

MEETING YOUR FEAR

Right from the start, Lisa faced a complex tangle of fears head-on. In this early stage, you will be dealing with fear. Fear takes many forms, but at this point in the journey, if a partner has died or left, most people's greatest fear takes the form of being afraid to be alone. The fear of being alone in the early days can be unbearable, and it can feel as though your independent nature will simply dissolve, pulling you down into a whirlpool of emotion until you slip below the surface and become lost.

For many of the women I work with, a common form this fear takes is the question: *What will I do without sex?* This was certainly a question I had initially. I was in the sexual prime of my life at forty-three, and post-traumatic stress was settling in places in my body I could not understand. This pent-up sexual energy would continue to penetrate my thoughts about how I was going to deal with that part of my life, as I had enjoyed a fulfilling sexual relationship with my husband for twenty-five years. You will deal with these questions in time, but for now, the most important thing is to know that this is the kind of fear to be watchful of reacting to. It's tempting to go right out and fill that gap with another relationship in search of love. But that act would simply delay facing the fear that awaits your attention.

So many will urge you to reenter quickly—to get out of grief fast, making grief your enemy. Grief is not the villain here; grief has shown up to heal you. Grief is an emotional response to loss—a friend that visits you for a time to assist you into your feeling space, in order to empty all that gets sequestered to a darkened room to lie dormant, waiting if not attended to.

The American Buddhist teacher Pema Chödrön has long pointed the way to finding peace on the hero's journey—always with a vulnerable willingness to talk about, face, and touch the hand of fear; always encouraging her students and readers to sit with their fear, let it be there, not make it into more than what it is. I think Pema beautifully summarized this point in the journey when she said, "Like all explorers, we are drawn to discover what's out there without knowing yet if we have the courage to face it."

When you go through heartbreak, you are sitting with what was always in you, which could be loneliness, anger, shame, and, yes, fear. But this is your opportunity to go to and through that bottom-line feeling and peel back layers of the onion skin of that protection. While it brings up fear to be so raw, a healthy way to heal is to think, *Oh, I get to feel what this feels like now without suppression, and I get to move through it. And something will replace it once I move through it.* As you place your intention on being present as you are feeling vulnerable, you are receptive to the feelings that come. Please know that whatever that big, daunting feeling is, something always replaces it. Fear may be in the field right now, but allow it to pass. It will pass, as everything does. *This too shall pass.* I repeat this phrase often and will do so many times in the coming pages. These words are so comforting. This anger, this fear, this despair will pass. The light will come as you feel to heal.

Take a moment with me now, if you can, to drop into stillness. Take a deep breath in, and let it out slowly . . . and now see yourself standing at the mouth of an estuary, where the powerful ocean tides meet the river current of your life. Allow yourself to find comfort in this primordial meeting place, a reminder that no matter how insistent the voices of fear can be at times, you are not separate from the source of all life. You are both the sea and the tributaries that flow into it. And as you are preparing to begin your hero's journey, you are indeed finding your way back to the flow where there's no paddling upstream with resistance. I always say, "Save the swimming upstream for the salmon to do."

REDESIGNING YOUR LIFE FOR HEALING

This crisis has brought you to a place called the change curve. You may have gone through the shock and disbelief, and now you have to pivot and turn toward the journey. That means that the first thing you have to do is redesign your life. That may be happening naturally. You break up, and you have to leave your apartment. You lose your job, and suddenly you're looking for a new job. Your house burns down, and you have to find a new place. You will naturally find yourself on a new course, going in a direction that you did not foresee. But you must understand that the first true step on the hero's journey is to consciously change *how* you live your life. The quality of the choices and decisions you make next will determine how this path unfolds.

In this stage, you are already facing the next choices, and I want to give you tools for getting through. I want you to think of this time as entering into a protective cocoon of healing where it can be messy while you create space for yourself however you can—even if it's finding the quiet mental space of safe sanctuary inside that you need. Many of these choices you will make feel very practical. You are probably overwhelmed with details. While you may wish to remain in your protected and safe nest at home, there are a thousand baby steps you need to prepare to take to move forward. Even as I was swimming deep into an ocean of grief, I faced the plans for Richard's memorial service and met with the principals of my girls' schools to make a plan for them to get the support to continue their studies despite everything else that was happening. Eventually I had to deal with details like selling Richard's car and organizing the paperwork for our estate. These may sound mundane, but they are a huge part of everyone's experience at this point in a journey of loss, and they provide an early opportunity to use the power of making choices to inform the path you will take.

When Lisa learned that she had cancer, she went through her own heartbreak at realizing the loss of her health. Suddenly, she went from being normal to being a woman with cancer who's going to lose all of her hair. As she grieved, so did she shift into action. She instantly became a master of making life-affirming choices. She did it in her own way, making choices that were significant and empowering for *her*, even when the people around her, those who love her deeply, didn't fully understand.

There are four practices that will help you to redesign your life in ways that will support the healing and flowering of your body, mind, and spirit. They will help to keep you on track, even when your heart is aching and you're not feeling confident about your next steps. These practices will also aid you in cultivating the hero's mindset that will serve you well for the rest of your life.

- *Making time and space for healing*
- *Prioritizing your needs*
- *Aligning with supreme self-care*
- *Practicing mindfulness*

Making Time and Space for Healing

The first step is to make the time and space for healing to happen, to design your life specifically for your unique process. A part of that is designing the space for your grief and for feeling in general. The redesigning that you're doing at this stage is mostly an internal process, which the other three practices support in a big way, but there are also aspects of your outer world that you might choose to reshape in some ways. For example, you could do a cleanse of your calendar and create the space you need for the quality of reflection as you block out time that will reconnect you with yourself. You might choose to clean out clutter in a closet to rid yourself of what you no longer want or need, clearing and tidying your physical space so that you can better sense and feel your own inner rhythm. You might also want to look around your home—and consider places in nature that you love, too—and go with the gravitational pull to the spaces that feel like your own healing cocoons.

As for time, I encourage you to not overbook and overschedule your life right now. Clarity doesn't come in busyness; it comes when you're aligned with change.

Prioritizing Your Needs

It's time to look at your life and ask yourself essential questions: *What do I need now? How am I going to get it, do it, find it, ask for it? Do I need a friend, or a team of friends? Do I need a lover? Do I need a partner or assistant at work or at home?* Each time I asked myself these questions, my barometer was: *Can this person hold me without fixing me?* My friend Christina Rasmussen, a real hero, in her book *Second Firsts: Live, Laugh, and Love Again,* poignantly describes how she needed her parents to leave her alone in the early stages after her husband's death. This meant that they would return to Greece while she tended to her children and her grieving process in a private way. Finding her own footing was one of the things she needed. If you just tune in to yourself, you know exactly what you need. Identify what you need. Ask for it. Insist on it. What support do you need? Is it to ask people to give you space or to come in closer? Or is it both?

Aligning with Supreme Self-care

Aligning with supreme self-care begins with being gentle and compassionate and with treating your body really well—long salt baths, quiet music, meditation, hot tea. It can also include spending time in nature in wide-open spaces, limiting your use of drugs and alcohol, and finding healthy ways to give yourself quiet time as a reprieve from your busy schedule. Supreme self-care, of course, also includes the practices we just covered—asking for support from friends, if that's what you need, and sometimes asking for space. Your time spent in nature will nourish and sustain you in remarkable ways in the coming days. One of the reasons for this is that nature organically provides the wide-open space that is so healing and renewing. There is soul energy in trees, and so much beauty to be held in. When one of my close friends was going through a divorce, he took long walks in nature almost daily for the first few months. I recently met a new friend while speaking at Outessa, an outdoor event for women sponsored and run by REI: Karla Amador. This remarkable woman cofounded a global movement in the process of taking space and taking care of herself during her divorce. It's called the 52 Hike Challenge, an organization that now inspires others to do what she did: hiking once a week for an entire year as a way to heal the mind, body, and soul by walking and breathing through the pain of loss to reclaim life.

Practicing Mindfulness

Suffering has a way of rocking our world and bringing us straight into mindfulness. In her powerful TED Talk titled "The Power of Mindfulness," Dr. Shauna Shapiro says, "Perfection isn't possible, but transformation is. All of us have the capacity to change, to learn, to grow, no matter what our circumstances." We must embrace this mindfulness for the journey ahead. Mindfulness is embodying our aliveness with full awareness and a kind of gentle and compassionate attention to how we are feeling. Mindfulness is so much more than a technique. It's about having a love affair with life: embracing the good, the bad, and the ugly with gentle compassion and the intention of kindness in the present moment. It is possible to remain in love with life—even as you are going through the unfathomable.

Preparing for the journey with mindfulness means not numbing out—not drinking too much, not working too much, unplugging as much as possible. Be specific about the kind of things that you want to put your attention on, and go looking for inspiration. As a deep awareness practice, mindfulness helps you to tune in to your body. What does your body need? How is your body expressing the pain that you're in? How can you be in tune with that? You have a healer inside that will speak to you—often through pain, tension, anxiety, or discomfort—but you have to listen. You must tune in to your body and all that it tells you.

THE SOUL INQUIRY:
GOING DEEPER IN

Oftentimes it's when everything falls apart that life can begin to come together. Your heart breaks, shatters into a million pieces, and when it comes back together it's bigger. It's expanded. There is more depth, more love, in a heart that is re-forming at an even greater capacity. This Soul Inquiry session is dedicated to your expanding heart. The questions in this chapter will reveal to you how you are preparing and stepping into your new life, embracing loss.

1. What is your "message in the mess"? Your message in the mess is the essence of what you have learned from this heartbreak—your great "aha moment" of crystal clarity.
2. Why has this experience shown up for you now? What is it here to teach you?
3. What are some of your greatest fears at this time?
4. How has grief shown up? Are you acknowledging your grief and making space to feel it?

Your New Story • *transformational writing process*

As you embark on this journey of healing, how can you best prepare for it? Do certain parts of your life need to be redesigned to support your healing? What are your greatest needs right now, and how will you make time and space to prioritize them? What new supreme self-care practices will you adopt now? What type of mindfulness practice will you benefit from the most? Write a preparation plan that feels supremely good to you.

_____

_____

_____

_____

_____

_____

_____

_____

_____

_____

_____

_____

_____

_____

_____

_____

_____

_____

_____

Chapter 3

Awakening

The Promise of Chapter 3—It's time to feel again. The walls around your heart are coming down, and grief is beckoning you to trust what happens when you allow the flow of your deepest and most authentic emotions to come forward. Your feelings are your medicine—and they will heal you all the way through. In your own sacred timing, your heart is awakening to feel your life.

Dustin DiPerna is an extraordinary meditation teacher and religious scholar whom I had the joy of interviewing not long ago for my podcast. Very quickly in our short time together, we went straight to the heart of the matter, and he shared this about awakening to life through the pain of loss:

Suffering can become a portal to a sea of interconnectedness, because in our own suffering we begin to realize that if we make it personal—and of course aspects of suffering are personal and remain personal—but if we make it only personal, then through suffering we feel isolation. But there's a possibility to allow suffering to open your heart. There's a sense of recognizing that your own suffering is something that's shared by many, many others. Loss of a loved one, loss of a parent, loss of a child, loss of a friend—these types of loss are actually experiences of part of what it means to be a human being and alive on our planet. And if we can use our suffering as a portal to come into contact with others who are also experiencing something similar—certainly not the same, because every situation is unique, but something similar—it allows us to feel a deeper sense of connection to the people around us and to other people who are experiencing it. And so, as words of hope, if you take the suffering without trying to deny it or trying to run away from it, but if you actually allow yourself to feel it, there is a pathway that can break your heart open and can allow you to be in contact with an interconnected sea of humanity who's also experiencing that. And that feeling then transforms the suffering into connection, and into hope and possibility—and it's a pathway that is open to anyone.

In many countries around the world, death and loss are aspects of everyday life. Along the banks of the Ganges River in India, or one of its many tributaries, you will see families and friends gathered each and every day around the funeral pyre of a beloved one who has died. The full cycle of life isn't hidden. Mortality is a part of ordinary life. More commonly in third-world countries than in the West, people live with the realization that everything is temporary, and this understanding brings with it a more potent culture of gratitude among the people—young and old alike. The ephemeral nature of life is the greatest message in the mess for all of humanity. The beauty of loss for every one of us is the opportunity to wake up and engage more fully with life, so we feel connected heart to heart to everything and everyone—so the beauty of life is not only seen, it is felt.

Now is the time to awaken to the heart, experiencing the full range of your emotions, rather than to become closed down—stuck and embittered. Now is the time to be a hero who chooses to be broken wide open, rather than be a victim who chooses to shut down.

The beauty of any awakening is that the walls come down from around your heart to allow you to be more fully engaged and connected to the present moment. Life does its work on us, to bring us home in ourselves to feel the full capacity of the heart. In loss, for many the awakened heart is very alive—feeling the grief, yes, and also feeling *all* of life. You may feel more sensitized to everything in this state of heightened awareness. As my own wall came down in those early months of loss, it felt like a pressurized water hose hitting me in the face—I realized for the first time that I had been asleep to my feelings. With Richard's death, I found myself seeing life with new eyes, like a newborn baby. Everything was brighter and more beautiful and more ecstatic. It was as though life continued to call me into it, inviting me to partake in the feast of beauty that I had awakened to . . . and I remain awake to this day. This is a major pivot— when you realize there's no going back to sleep. When this happens to you—and it happens at different times for each of us and is sparked by various circumstances—it is always your soul that calls to you to awaken. Perhaps only the soul knows why and when you are open enough to embrace this beautiful time—that can often happen amidst suffering. Once you are awakened, it's a new beginning, and you see the world more clearly with new vision. If this seems like a big leap from where you are in this moment, I ask that you stay with me; this book can be your bridge. If you choose to walk the hero's path, you are going to awaken.

LOOSENING THE GRIP OF GUILT, ANGER, RESENTMENT, AND REGRET

As the wall comes down, the time of awakening is a sacred opening that reveals the unhealthy ego and allows us to turn toward it, to see what this wounded and afraid part of us has made of our relationships and of our lives. Despite itself, it has put an illusion resembling safety above all else—above growth, expansion, and freedom. It clings to the relationship you had with the marriage, the job, the body, the self-image—the life you had, which is no longer. The ego creates suffering by identifying with attachment to some aspect of life that you have lost, and here's how the quality of your thinking plays a role in your recovery.

For me, ego and unhealthy ego are best defined by the ways we create our identity—both the healthy and unhealthy beliefs about who we are. Our beliefs can make up a story that builds a wall around the heart, separating us from who we *really* are—and from others as well. Our thoughts come and go in our minds, like breathing, and sometimes we latch on to them like sticky tape. In this process of latching on, we engage our suffering over and over. Like a well-rehearsed script, many of these thoughts come together to form a pattern; it becomes a habit to be on this train of thought. As you picture a train moving along the tracks, going on a journey, each individual car on the train represents your thoughts, all connected—all taking you to a destination. This train can take you far away from the present moment into desolate land where you are isolated from others. When you finally get off the train of thought, how are you feeling? Your feelings are your best navigation tool for showing you the itinerary of your thinking mind. They will also tell you who is the conductor—you or your ego. Once you notice how you are feeling on this train of thought, will you choose this same destination again? Or perhaps you will see that the tracks have been laid in your brain to go there by habit. This is where you can consciously choose earlier next time to get off the train, simply by noticing and asking sooner: *How am I feeling right now?* Breathe into this awareness and come back to the present moment. Boom! You're off that track and experiencing other thoughts that are bringing you home to your body—home to where you are—home to yourself and the life that is happening, and most important, out of your ego mind that causes you to suffer.

Now is when you are most raw. It's also when the potential for opening and healing is greatest. With these circumstances, the unhealthy ego is dying a death as its lifeline to a long-standing identity has disappeared; in some cases there is a complete annihilation and loss of identity. You are cracked open, raw and vulnerable like a splayed fish out of water. When you're in survival, you are most awake. One day you were living your life, and then your initiation happened and changed everything.

Kate was in her twenties when she was brutally attacked in her bed one night. A serial rapist had broken into her apartment, and she fought for her life and won. As she shared her story of the attack with me, what prominently stuck out for her was how she felt in those first few days after the attack: the aliveness, the amazement, the gratitude, the feeling of living without a skin—having been so close to the doorway between life and death. She survived a brutal attack, her brush with death, and was awakened to the precious gifts of life. Therein lies the paradox—and the beauty of awakening through suffering on the hero's journey.

This time of awakening offers an escape route, a chance to get unstuck from the thought patterns that by old habit may be keeping you where you are. This is also where the ego will coil like a snake and strike, with thoughts that seem to come out of nowhere and cause all manner of suffering. These thoughts are often confining and dispiriting, and, if left unattended, will build that wall back up around your heart, numbing you to your feelings and impeding your growth. You must peel back the onion and witness your own thoughts—becoming the observer of your thinking and further strengthening the depth of awareness that is central to the hero's mindset. What does this mean? Let me tell you the story of Sue, a woman I met who was also dealing with the loss of her husband. Sue's husband had died five years earlier, but even though so much time had passed, she told me that she still felt her pain as acutely as if her husband's death had happened yesterday. What I now know is that Sue's situation is all too common: What she perceived as unending pain was a screen for endlessly repeating thought patterns that kept her stuck. She replayed her "what if" thoughts over and over, keeping her stuck in her victim thinking and in survival mode for five years. The more we talked, the more we were able to peel back the layers and dig into what was happening under the surface. In particular, Sue suffered from a sense of survivor's guilt. She felt she should have been able to see her husband's illness coming—if not to save him, then to prepare herself. She felt regret for things she had said and things she hadn't said while her husband was still alive. These feelings are entirely natural, and the important thing at this stage is to recognize the chaos present in heartbreak and transformation. Eventually you will be able to address and heal these recurring thoughts, letting them soften and become like clouds passing by, and the inner-world conversation becomes like white noise that fades into the background. For now, the important step is to simply peel back the onion and awaken to the raw emotions that manifest from the thoughts.

This is the time to surrender to what you're feeling and trust it so that you can get unstuck from the grief, guilt, regrets, and other repeating spinning gears that create thought patterns that hold you back. As part of your life-school curriculum, you are learning the art of noticing and observing what's present for you. You can begin to pull back the layers now to feel and see what's happening underneath, and I'm here to help you.

THE CHOICE TO BECOME BITTER OR BETTER

I was standing in line outdoors under the PAY HERE window of my local gas station when Krystal walked up. I hadn't bumped into her in a long time. Our daughters had played together and often had sleepovers. Krystal and her husband, Rob, were college sweethearts, but they didn't have a "happy" marriage, although they tried to make it work for the kids. Rob bolted when their oldest daughter graduated from high school, leaving Krystal for a new relationship. Krystal, now divorced, faced me as I greeted her in line. I almost gasped as she blurted out, "You know, Kris, I think it's almost easier if your husband dies."

Krystal's pronouncement spoke volumes about her pain and deep anger at being left alone. She carries the weight of bitterness, but it was always her anger that caused the angst in her marriage—and ultimately all sorts of problems with her self-esteem and image. For Krystal, peeling back the onion reveals layers of bitterness that make her feel very much like the victim of her divorce. Krystal's crucible of transformation is to observe these recurring thoughts and recognize that her marriage was over long before Rob walked out the door. Whether she chooses to become vulnerable about her feelings or not, this is her initiation into a new story and her opportunity of awakening.

There are times when anger helps us to catalyze change, and, of course, if someone cheats on you, breaching their commitment to your relationship, it hurts and you will feel angry. Or if you have left an abusive relationship, you may carry both shame and anger. Sitting in a circle with women at a retreat, I was surprised by how many of them had suffered from an abuser. A couple of the women, now healed and well on their way, still had not forgiven themselves for allowing that relationship to continue for so long before they escaped. They both carried shame for having stayed too long and anger that this person mistreated and manipulated them into staying. These women need to process both forgiveness of self and forgiveness of other.

It might seem easier in a breakup to be angry than to break up and still feel those comfortable and familiar feelings of love. But what if the relationship has run its course and served you both well, but you've just outgrown it? You can leave in love without hate and anger. It may feel more difficult to let go at first, but as you forgive yourself and the other, it's easier to let go in love than to be bound by anger and hate. Forgiveness is a gift you give yourself by letting go of the story that takes up your headspace and ties you to negative feelings. When you can love the person while letting go, it's a much gentler process that allows you to feel positive, good feelings while you move through being sad that things didn't work out for you both. You can remain loving and kind and hold that relationship dear to you with respect for what you shared. We must become more comfortable as a culture with the idea that love is more powerful than hate and anger. Expel your anger, forgive, and let go, and you will be free and filled with love.

When our girls were young, Melissa came to be our live-in family helper while going to graduate school in psychology at a nearby university. You wouldn't have known it, because her cheerful personality and bright inner light hid that she had gone through unimaginable pain and suffering, but already in the course of her young life of twenty-three years, she had been raped three times. Given what happened to her in later years, another person might have felt attacked by life. Her husband suffered a massive stroke, and then her son was diagnosed with cancer. Even though Melissa was thrown curveball after curveball, she never faltered in her faith. She found laughter amidst her tears. She remained awake. I marveled at how she continued to allow her light to shine after having lived through such dark circumstances.

One of Melissa's first life-altering incidents happened years earlier when she was in Paris and going to school on an exchange program. She answered an ad to get some language tutoring. When she arrived at the apartment listed in the ad, everything went terribly wrong. Melissa was held captive by her assailant for three days, raped repeatedly, and treated like an animal. I asked her how she got through it, and she said that for those three days he had looked at her like an animal, an object to be tortured. She didn't dare look at him for fear that the violence would further escalate. On the third day, she pleaded with him in a way that allowed him to see her humanity. She had somehow penetrated his sociopathic lens, and he let her go. "Get the fuck out of here" was all he said. Her amygdala brain in full fight-or-flight mode, she knew she had one window and it would close very quickly, and so she fled her captivity like a rabbit running from fright in the night.

Melissa ran for her life—and kept going. Leaving most of her stuff behind, she packed a travel bag and left the country. She didn't call her parents and tell them of the attack. They didn't even know that she'd quit her exchange program. Melissa, at nineteen years old, in shock and disbelief, and without a fully developed prefrontal cortex at that age, reasoned that if she could just pretend that the incident didn't happen, then it didn't happen. She didn't tell the police; she did not speak of what had happened to her until many years later. She finally realized that her own mind now held her captive in fear and that she would never stop running until she confronted her internal demons. It took her years to finally tell her family and open the door to her healing.

When Melissa came to stay with us, she lived in our guesthouse, which we began to recognize as a place of healing. Others had come there to heal, too—to be held in that loving family space where the hope for a better life became a poignant possibility. We didn't do anything particularly special to it. It was a small room and bath with a kitchenette and separate entrance, attached to the house. The space just healed them, and our love was a potent balm to broken hearts mending. Melissa shared with me one day that her interactions with Richard were also part of her healing. She said that he was the first man she felt completely safe being around. He held her as a brother would, and she felt protected in a way that made her realize that not all men were going to hurt her.

Putting miles and years between herself and her traumas didn't lessen the brutal impact. Melissa was trying valiantly to live her life, but her unattended emotions burdened her greatly—especially limiting her ability to trust and to relate to men. A long vow of silence and living in denial didn't make the hurt any less true—or heal the wound or drive the fear away. No matter how safe and steady it can appear to be, the path of denial is not the hero's journey. Denial can be a momentary tourniquet to stanch the bleeding of a ravaged heart, as emotional first aid. But the hero's journey is one that insists on truth-telling . . . and this time of awakening blows the doors wide open to doing just that.

WHAT WE RESIST IN THE WAKE OF DENIAL

Whatever has happened to you, you have to make it real. Richard walked out the door and never returned. I knew that I had to make it real right away and that denial would be a very dangerous place to live.

At one of my retreats, I met Lucy, a deep-feeling woman who was wrestling with the losses of her mother and one of her brothers. Lucy was one of five siblings, three girls and two boys. One of her younger brothers had died in a car accident six years earlier at the age of thirty-five. Lucy's mom, Carol, never regained her footing after her son died, and on the fifth anniversary of his death decided life wasn't for her any longer. Lucy described how she was caught in a terrible cycle, suffering with images in her mind of her mom's lifeless body hanging by her neck—this beautiful, joyous woman who was deeply loved dangling lifeless like a rag doll. With our retreat group as her safe container, she wondered aloud with a question that I believe has stirred in most of us: Why can't some make it through the pain long enough to gain perspective—long enough to pause that one permanent decision that can never be turned back?

There came a point in her grieving process when Lucy began to judge her mother's decision and could only feel anger: anger at her choice to leave this message for her lineage; anger that she could abandon her husband, children, grandchildren, and great-grandchildren with such a memory imprinted on their souls. Knowing that her mother's demons rose and subsided over the years, Lucy had always feared she might do this, especially after losing her beloved son, but that didn't change that one elongated moment that shook Lucy with shock at the stark reality of death once again.

In Carol's small but tidy home studio lay her reading glasses, paintbrushes, photos, and books, all where she left them. One might question her last moments—how she could say good-bye to life that way. It's so different when someone dies of natural causes, because deep down, you know they wanted to live more life. For someone with good health and a strong body to end her life twenty years prematurely—I think it's hard for most of us to relate to that level of pain. Lucy said that she always thought that her mom suffered from not having the spiritual connection that makes the journey so rich. If one cannot see beyond the pain to value the tremendous journey of life, then loss can easily be heart-closing instead of heart-opening. There are times for all of us when we just want the pain to stop. And denial can act like cement, sometimes fully paving over the possibility of healing. Getting past pain—moving through the shadow—deepening the understanding of what it means to love life more than all else is the way.

The danger of denial is that you would never step into the heroic path of your healing journey that you are made for. You would always remain in shock and disbelief, surviving inside the glass snow globe of the illusion of a life that no longer exists. It's a way of remaining a victim instead of acknowledging that it's real. In my years struggling with an eating disorder, I knew all too well that denial was a dangerous place to inhabit, where I would not acknowledge the truth of what I was doing to myself and where I remained a victim of my ego mind. Denial could turn days into weeks and weeks into months as months rolled into years of life passing by. I knew this would be true for me if I didn't face Richard's death head-on—immediately. I decided to take it upon myself to phone all of his closest friends. One name after another, beginning in the *A*'s and moving through to *Z* in his address book, I spent hours letting his friends know what had happened. I repeated one hundred times the story that Richard had died. I did so to make it real for me. I knew that otherwise I might always be waiting for him to return.

Although these words can be offered too soon after a loss, eventually we see a path to wholeness in embracing what is as opposed to resisting what is. Resistance to me always represents the path of suffering. Surrendering to what is represents the path of growth, empowerment, moving forward, turning toward, and moving toward the light. It's the empowered choice. Denial is a very disempowering place to live, whether you're denying the truth of what you're doing with your life, how someone has mistreated you, your addiction, or a relationship that you and your partner keep up only out of fear of not being in each other's lives—and long after it has already started to die a long, slow death, when you are already no longer connected. There can be a lot of pain in that, and most of us midlifers have experienced a modicum of denial taking different forms in our lives. There is a deep loneliness when you're disconnected but in denial about that. It happens a lot—denying to yourself when there is a lack of intimacy and little connection with the person sitting next to you.

Denial sits like a glacier, sliding ever so slowly, nearly imperceptibly, over the pain that we don't think we will survive. Some part of us decides that numbness will suffice, at least for a while.

FEEL TO HEAL

One of the things that was most evident and shocking to me in loss was the contrast to how numb I had been living in my normal other life—the one that ended with Richard's death. The wall around my heart that I had unknowingly and innocently grown to barricade my feelings had shattered, and suddenly I could feel everything.

After those first waves of grief, there was only one other experience that felt oddly similar that I could relate to, and that was the inner process I had designed to open in natural childbirth—diving deep inward, dealing with my pain, to give birth to my daughters. I intuited that I was giving birth again, and I would need to design life differently to go through a process of healing that would be the first stage of my hero's journey. For women and men alike, there is an innate understanding that when we open more to feeling our emotions, there can be waves of pain that ripple through us, sensations that are more intense than we may believe we can endure. But we breathe. And we make it through.

As my process deepened and my path became clear, I allowed my days to make room to feel in order to heal, to allow myself the space and time to go in as well as to come out of these waves of loss. After the girls left for school, I would lie in bed or on the floor and allow myself just to be wherever I happened to be emotionally. I breathed. I checked in. I noticed where my body held tension. I began to identify my body's language, often spoken through pain. I allowed my body's intelligence to show me the way out.

I would spend time in silence. I had no stimulus—no radio, no television. I was selective in my reading, too; I read poetry. I gently exercised and spent time every day in nature. Hiking and fresh air were really good for me, especially when I was low. Sometimes I would sit on the floor listening to music and just let my body move. I was sensitive to all voices. Everything triggered me: song lyrics, the world news, and the words of every story. I felt it all.

Grief is a determined advocate for emptying your feelings, giving voice to even those feelings you believe to be most ineffable. Expel what is eating away at you to be expressed. These feelings will not leave you any other way—they will remain dormant as they grow from sadness to something else if avoided or rejected. Here is where your choice is: Will you go into them now—or will you feel them later?

I remember one morning when I lay completely surrendered and open on my bedroom floor. I cried and screamed and kicked my legs. I beat the bedroom pillows as I allowed grief to open me. I breathed. I cried again. I felt wasted. My body thanked me for letting it all out by replacing tension with peace. As the pain had subsided, I felt something akin to bliss.

I walked outside and felt the cool breeze dry my salt-teared face. I could feel life in every leaf of the oak trees and every blade of grass. The colors of the sky were like a Rembrandt, and I noticed the cloud formations and red sky at night. Suddenly, I could feel life everywhere—and I realized I had been living asleep to all the beauty that surrounds me.

As I surrendered more and more to the grief and to my tears, my body began to change as well. It was strange. Something shifted, and a youthful vitality returned. During this time I looked years younger. It turns out, crying is a natural youth elixir that boosts the immune system. Medical journals galore document that repressed emotions weaken our immunity, which sets off a cascade of stress hormones circulating through the body. Counteracting those deleterious effects, emotional tears have higher levels of potassium, manganese, and other essential nutrients that sweep away the aging chemicals. I visited a massage therapist twelve weeks after my first surrender. She exclaimed, "Wow, Kris! I have never seen your neck so loose, and your shoulders have completely opened in the back. Have you been doing a lot of yoga or something?"

My body was opening my heart and teaching me how to feel and let go. Grief was not my enemy but a friend showing up for a time as it allowed me the healthy means to feel and express the pain inside me. I became more adept at anticipating and surrendering sooner to my feelings. I learned to read my emotions by the signals from my body. At first it was hours a day, but over time the cycles shortened. I would sometimes have reprieve days, often two- or three-day cycles before grief would return. And when it did, each wave would pass in and out, and always rewarding me with a sense of peace at its completion.

"This too shall pass" continued to be a mantra for me. Intuitively, I understood that listening to my body and how it talked to me would be my path back to a new life. I also knew I needed to redesign my life to include spaciousness that allowed stillness. I needed to create time and space for just being quiet—mindful only of my breath and where I could allow all those feelings of confusion, regret, fear, longing, and anger to surface and be expelled through grief. I learned I didn't have to be afraid of where my feelings might lead me, because it was all inside me and part of the carefully woven fabric of healing. I just had to follow the thread of my feelings right into my broken heart mending.

Creating the space to move in and out of whatever came was essential to my healing. I learned to surrender and to allow mind, body, and spirit to integrate. I discovered that as a gust of wind forces the door open wide, so did grief awaken my heart.

GLIMPSES OF LIGHT

My friend Lisa was breathtakingly awake to all of her journey. Sure, when she heard the news that she had breast cancer she was in shock and disbelief, but she didn't remain there long. During her cancer treatments of months of chemotherapy, she was especially grateful for the days she felt good, so grateful for the reprieve in her cycles of healing from chemicals. She knew that a week later she would go into her cocoon of her own choice after chemo. She was acutely awake when she felt good. She would actually celebrate: "Oh my God, I feel good! I'm going to go out to lunch!" Or, "I am going to arrange flowers today"—all the while knowing that she would be feeling terrible soon enough. Lisa had been more than moderately health-conscious all of her life, and now she was having to put chemicals into her body, "killing" herself in a way in order to live. The journey through grief and healing often can feel counterintuitive as well. Just as Lisa surrendered (counterintuitive to her healthy life practices) to her treatments and lived through the ill effects, our loss has knocked us down, and we need to get up and face the feelings that come. But instead of doing battle with them in resistance, we must surrender and succumb to those feelings. Lying spread-eagle on the floor is how I surrendered to grief. Counterintuitive to my brain's response to fight or take flight in fear, my body-positioned vulnerability in a five-pointed star as I lay on the floor shaking is how I found my feelings, released them, and received peace.

You may very well wish to run right out and fill that enormous hole in your broken heart—with another relationship, or a move to a new city, or a trip to a faraway land. And it may feel counterintuitive to just sit with the feelings as they are and not fill them with a temporary need that comes in the form of a distraction from healing what's broken. If you follow the path of temporarily filling your empty space with something or someone, I will tell you from experience that it can be a longer transition, where broken attracts broken, and that neediness can be a rough start to love. Herein lies the power of the ego mind and those thoughts you have about being alone; fear can become a driving factor when you are already in such pain. As I learned that leaning into fear is living awake, there were times it would become exhausting. So I would find comfort and rest in my lover's arms for a time. (Yes, I did say *lover.*)

In hindsight, I wished I had been able to sit on my own longer and had been less broken before I started dating. And, in the end, there is never any wasted time spent learning and growing, soul to soul, as we do in all kinds of loving relationships—even those that are meant to be transitional. Love is always a stealthy teacher, and all relationships are a reflection of us at that time in our lives. But a new love can be the healing balm to your broken heart and help you move forward. Or sitting a bit in celibacy can also be your way to heal. It's your choice.

If you have lost a partner, you probably felt that you needed this other person in order to be whole and complete. But truly, that is one of the biggest illusions of all told by your unhealthy ego. You *are* whole and complete as you are, in your essence. Sometimes we think we have fallen in love, but depending on where we are in ourselves, feeling broken or whole, what we have fallen in is need. It looks like love and feels passionate because sometimes what we need is to feel alive. This relationship represents a transitional bond and feels like a soul-mate connection. In those desperate heartbroken waves, a new love can become a Band-Aid for a wound that really needs a tourniquet.

We long for something to be filled in us that we can only fill ourselves. While a lover may be a balm to your heartache, I would warn you not to look to another to fulfill you, because it's an impossibility. If you are looking to another for something that is only to be healed, discovered, and recovered on your own, your search will be frustrating and confusing. You were born whole and complete, and you've bought into believing or have been taught otherwise, but your journey will soon bring you to a place where your soul will know the truth.

Life appears to be relentlessly optimistic, even in the wake of the worst things. Like a hope-filled lover who won't give up, it's always asking us to give it another chance. It's asking us to live—and to at least consider opening the heart instead of shutting it down. In this time of awakening, allow all of your feelings to come forward. Your sadness and sorrow; your anger and resentment; your guilt, doubt, and distrust—all of these once released will eventually awaken you to your joy, too. As part of your awakening, you must become wide open and accept the divine invitation that has come from this initiatory event to grow. What is spirit calling you to do?

For me, the call of spirit was to retreat into the wilderness of nature and also to travel the world. I had to ignite the spirit of adventure so that I could come back home again and return to the reality of healing. I couldn't have come back to stillness and the inner world of going deeper without leaving it first. I had a wanderlust for a while. I needed to prove to myself that I could manage alone. I took trips to India, Peru, Guatemala, and Costa Rica. I traveled alone, with my family, and with my friends. But this wanderlust only temporarily assuaged a deeper longing I could not understand at this stage of my healing. My yearning for all things that would make me feel more passionately alive was beginning to grow like a thirst one has in the desert. And today, I lead retreats for other women who are on this same stage of their journey. When you retreat from your everyday life, it becomes far easier to see and reflect on what needs to change, and the options you have become more obvious as you step away from your ordinary life. It's easier to receive more clarity about those deeper longings that are only stirrings that you shove aside in your daily life. These inklings will lead you and be your breadcrumbs to follow along the path of self-discovery.

SOUL MANTRA:

Please lie on the floor spread-eagle with your arms and legs stretched out in a five-pointed star. Breathe deeply, allowing your body full freedom to shake and let emotion rise, and repeat as long as you need to:

I surrender, trust, and accept. I allow myself to feel to heal.

THE SOUL INQUIRY:
OPEN TO YOUR AWAKENING

You can create miniretreats for yourself. Twenty or thirty minutes of quiet reflection and journaling with a cup of tea and a candle flickering in your periphery is good soul medicine. Or head out into nature, stopping along a favorite hiking trail to journal in the great outdoors. However you choose to do it, take some time now to practice presence, head into the gap, and become unbounded by thoughts so that you can receive greater wisdom and more creativity. Please pull out your journal and answer these questions.

1. What are you feeling? Are you feeling wounded, angry, betrayed, hurt, or another emotion?
2. Are you allowing yourself all of your feelings—the full range?
3. How do you express your feelings? Words, tears, screams, laughter, movement?

4. Can you see evidence of being in resistance or denial right now?
5. What part of your "old" life has your ego most strongly identified with?
6. Can you change this circumstance, whatever it is—the circumstance of this breakup or this devastating news you've received?

Your New Story • *transformational writing process*

This time of awakening finds you at another powerful choice point. Will you choose to become *better* from this loss? Or will you choose to be bitter? Will you break open or shut down? If you are stuck, write about why you are stuck. Is it anger, a refusal to grieve, or fear of change? What is spirit calling you to *do* to awaken your heart? How can you create space for more stillness in order to open and surrender to your heart?

_____

_____

_____

_____

_____

_____

_____

_____

Chapter 4

The Jagged Edge of Growth

The Promise of Chapter 4—You will feel guided into your growth. You will be able to face all of your obstacles, knowing that your growth depends on facing your fears and finding the reason for why things have shown up for you. This is where you begin to transform your story forever into the hero's journey.

Standing at the gate to my transatlantic flight on my way to the renowned Osho Path of Love workshop, this one taking place in Verona, Italy, I had a moment when I paused and consciously chose to move forward. I could have turned back as I faced the second obstacle that day, but something in me pressed forward, knowing in my heart that all would be OK. After all, I was on the path of love, I thought to myself, and I felt divinely inspired and protected.

Lisa and I had decided to embark on a spiritual adventure together. It was just eleven months after Richard's death, and I was about to come out in the public eye in tribute to him. I felt that a process like the Path of Love would be a good way to prepare my heart and mind. As I was on my way to the airport, I was moving my way up the OWN production line, interview by interview, for an appearance on *Oprah* scheduled one week after I would return from the workshop.

I knew I was too raw and uncensored to be traveling alone, and while Lisa had already participated in the Path of Love years earlier, she wanted to be by my side on this journey. We arrived at LAX and stood excitedly in line together. I placed my bags up on the weight scale and checked in, then moved to the right as Lisa placed her bags where mine had just disappeared around the corner on the winding belt that would take my bags to our plane. She began to leaf through her file folder and papers looking for her passport. With a panicked look in her eyes, she whispered, "Oh my God, oh my God, it's not here. It must have fallen out when I was in the ladies' room." As they removed her bags and placed them aside, I settled in a chair as Lisa raced back to retrace her steps. She came back with tears in her eyes and concern etched in her brow. "Kris, I can't find it. I can't believe this. I've ruined our trip."

It was an odd feeling I was having while waiting. I was more than my usual peaceful and calm. I had been on other spirit-driven trips, including pilgrimages to India to see the beloved spiritual teacher Sai Baba, and I knew that this "workshop" had already begun. It officially began when I made the choice to be there, and now my heart summoned me forward as I smiled and laughed. Making the moment lighter, I teased, "No, my friend, you've ruined your trip. I'm going, and I'll see you there. I believe I'm meant to step into this one alone."

This would be my very first solo trip away from my daughters, traveling to another world, and I felt its brevity in these moments. I waited as long as I could to go to my gate—maybe Lisa would find her passport. But she did not.

As I walked up to the business-class line, the attendant checked my ticket and said, "Miss, I'm sorry, you aren't seated in business class today. You are in economy plus." I retrieved my itinerary and confirmed that I had a business-class reservation, but somehow I'd been bumped to economy plus. I knew it was too late to fix this, as I had waited so long to board my flight. This is where I paused, noting that this was the second hiccup in my trip—first Lisa losing her passport, and now this mysterious seating change. I questioned for a moment, *Is the universe telling me to turn around and go home? To skip this trip? Or wait and get myself rebooked onto a different flight?* Whatever the universe was trying to communicate, I decided to keep moving forward.

As I got settled on the first leg of my trip, bound for London's Heathrow airport, I turned to the window to greet my fellow passenger. A few minutes later, as our plane took off, the younger man in his late twenties sitting next to me asked me a question with a thick country-English accent, in a tone that was very much like "Can you pass me that newspaper, please?" But this was a very unusual question: "Excuse me. You don't know anything about divine consciousness, do you?"

I'm sure I let out a giggle at the humor of spirit. Perhaps this is why my seat was switched. Perhaps the divine wanted me to have this conversation, because, of course, this was my language during that past year. I had been straddling between where Richard was in divine consciousness and where I was on the earth for nearly eleven months. I did, indeed, have a deep understanding of divine consciousness.

The man had been reading a book and handed it to me. It was an extremely heady book, which I leafed through as I shared my story of losing Richard, living in grief the past year, and all that I had learned from living in two dimensions and what I had discovered about the divine. We talked for a few hours—or mostly, I talked. I asked him a few questions about his stay in America. What was he doing here? He replied, "I was following Bruce Springsteen for six months while he was on tour." I queried back, *"Following?* You mean, like a groupie?" He sheepishly grinned. "Yeah, sort of."

People ask me now, did you notice anything different about him? I noticed that his social cues and responses to things were off, but then again, I wasn't myself either. I was off, too—wide-open emotionally and uncensored.

After the plane landed, I said good-bye to the man sitting next to me. As so often happens when we encounter someone on a train or plane, I assumed I'd never have contact with him again. We didn't exchange numbers. We didn't make any plans to keep in touch. I figured it had been a peculiar but interesting in-air conversation, and that was the end of it.

But that wasn't the end of it.

Here is where it's difficult to continue with this story, because what happened next didn't even feel like "real life." It felt more like a movie depicting one of the most ugly and evil displays of human behavior imaginable. What happened next is that this man from the plane began a seven-year-long cyberstalking campaign, terrorizing my family on an hourly basis, finally culminating in an international court case that ended with him in prison.

The entire experience was unbelievable, surreal, and yet there was no escape. I had to face the dragon. I had to protect my family. Emotionally, mentally, spiritually, I had to step into my power, calling on my fierce mother instincts, and become stronger in order to deal with this monster that hovered at the periphery of our lives every day.

Less than a year after Richard's death, still torn open with grief, I was about to find myself at the jagged edge of growth on this part of my journey—a very jagged edge indeed.

On the hero's path, after awakening to your life's mission, you will face many obstacles to challenge your new beliefs and way through life. Some of them may feel insurmountable. Although it may be difficult to remember in the moment, this is where surrender and trust in the journey itself really make you the hero. Sometimes, the dragon shows up to be the catalyst, and in this case, looking back, while I had been targeted by a serial stalker, I see now that I had refused to be his victim. Your dragon may be less dramatic than the one in this scenario, but it may also be seen as the catalyst of great change—something that has shown up to ignite the spark of your commitment to the hero's path.

It's difficult to explain to someone who has not been through such a protracted campaign of cyber stalking, bullying, and abuse what it's like to awaken every morning to be confronted by a text message from an unidentified internet platform that can't be blocked from "Stalker," an email, comments on Facebook, tweets from one of his multiple aliases, or negative comments posted following an interview or article I had contributed to someone else's website. Often, *all* of these platforms were used all day long with up to thirty aliases—all derived by one person determined to make his presence obvious through harassment. On the days when there wasn't a message, the uncertainty of where the next attack would come from weighed heavily on my mind. The only reprieve we received was when he slept for a few hours at night. Only then would my daughters and I receive a brief amount of time to mentally and physically catch our breath before he awoke and blasted his fire again.

The stalker carried out a carefully calculated and relentless campaign to damage my profile as an author. He had never met my younger daughter, but he became obsessed with the idea of marrying her, caught in a delusional web of his own imagining. He thought that if he harassed me enough I would concede to his demands to meet her in person. That shifted some years later as he began to demand up to £100,000 to stop his tactics. He was adept at using social media, constructing tweets and using hashtags that would cause someone searching for me on Twitter to potentially become exposed to his messaging on thousands of platforms to tens of thousands of people. Any person who contacted me in any way online would also be assaulted by him via social media. His tweets eventually became aimed at my fellow authors, at publishers, at media contacts, and at friends and family members, as well as all of my followers on social media. He chased them all on Twitter like a nasty virus, discouraging many of them from connecting with me. However, being an author in a day and age that requires an online community, I could not and would not distance myself from a public profile on the internet. I was determined to persevere despite this great wall of resistance I had to break through daily.

There was a time, before the FBI got involved, where I became fearful that he would turn up at book signings or public events that I was attending, and I limited our European travel, as I knew he lived in Wales. This restriction of movement was completely new to me.

Authors are not celebrities like movie stars. Prior to the internet and social media, Richard and I had our anonymity, living completely normal lives. The work we did in our book series was and is to inspire people to live happier, more fulfilling, and more peaceful lives. Outrageously, the stalker assumed my online identity, as well as stealing Richard's identity many times over the years, presenting himself as both of us all over the web. Before I knew about higher security in Facebook, he hacked into my Facebook account and retrieved personal messages as well as email lists of many of my contacts, including publishers, other authors, and media contacts, infiltrating my entire professional and personal network and emailing them as if he were me. During the peak of abuse, what the stalker often seemed to approach like a game was more like a slow-growing cancer to me, often taking six or more hours a day to manage and try to repair—all while supporting my daughters in their lives, working, and attempting to move forward in my personal life.

The physical safety of my family should not have been one of the primary concerns for us to deal with during the early years of sorrow after losing Richard, while grieving our loss—but it was. Security became an issue for our entire family. We began to feel unsafe even in our own home, despite the fact that the stalker was thousands of miles away. A parallel fact was that he had the capacity to jump on a plane to California and on numerous occasions expressed his intention to do that very thing—to come and meet his future bride and take her home to meet his family. He had sent flowers and gifts to my daughter at our home address, letting us know that he knew where we lived.

One night we received an email from the stalker telling us that his plane would soon be landing in our city. That same night, I received messages from my neighbors alerting me that someone was attempting to gain access into our community at the security gate.

After I called the police, I called on the help of a dear friend who immediately drove over, with his gun, and slept at our home that night for added security. Thankfully, it turned out to be a false alarm.

When the stalker actually did make the trip to the United States with the intention of meeting my daughter in person, I was terrified for our safety. I called the police and reported him, but they told me there would be nothing they could do until he came to my door. Well, I wasn't about to wait for that to happen. I employed the services of a Navy SEAL to protect us and our home while we frantically made our arrangements to leave the area. I evacuated my home, taking my daughter out of college temporarily. I knew when he left the area because the private investigator I had hired to track and confront him verified that he had indeed left San Francisco. I didn't feel safe any longer, and after considering what my options of protection were, I purchased a highly trained guard dog at a cost of $25,000. I issued a letter to my neighbors with a photo of the stalker, telling them of our situation and asking them not to let anyone in the gate who called from the entrance phone. I pursued recourse through the court system, even securing a court order in England. Despite all of this, it took years to halt the onslaught that stemmed from his delusional future with my daughter and his fixation with obtaining money from me. It was these years of hypervigilance that revealed something new to me about the woman I had grown into.

THE BIRTH OF A SPIRITUAL WARRIOR

Many nights I would toss and turn, unable to sleep, which sometimes inhibited my ability to be effective during the day in my business dealings. For my daughter, it was the same. The stress was unrelenting. I developed some nervous tics and twitches from hypervigilance, which have now subsided after several years without dealing with constant threat. I struggled with adrenal fatigue, hair loss, and thyroid dysfunction. Many of these health issues came as a result of the endless hours it required to capture and document all of the evidence in order to support my case—in order to free my family from this emotional and psychological abuse. While I consider myself a very resilient person, there were many times I was in tears and afraid; there were times I felt rage. In moments, it was a struggle to continue my work to inspire and guide others, as well as oversee the legacy of Richard's work amidst this tremendous test of adversity. I would often wake up in the middle of the night with nightmares and find it difficult to go back to sleep. Sometimes I'd have to jump out of bed and rage until I fell back to sleep, spent and exhausted.

There grew a weariness in my bones derived from years of "wrestling with the dragon" and his emotional torment. Along my own hero's path, there have been many bumps and bruises, and I'm sure you can account for yours during this vulnerable time as well. I'm certain that for all of us dealing with trauma, an exploration of the neuroscientific effects would show that feeling such long-term fear and living in fight-or-flight mode are unhealthy. Meditation helped to reduce some of the damage during this time and to manage increased cortisol levels—the primary stress hormone that can be damaging to the brain, the adrenal glands, and the overall hormonal system. Laughter became our way to deal with his torment as we did a daily check-in on who was the focus of his latest ridicule. We commented on the absurdity of his rash attacks, and we found ourselves in hysterics as often as we shed tears of frustration.

I did my best to keep it in perspective, but there were times when I felt panicked and scared. I had to protect my daughters. I had to protect myself. I also had to protect our entire *Don't Sweat the Small*

Stuff brand, as well as my future as an author who would need to utilize all of the social media platforms the stalker had breached. He made it extremely difficult for me to grow and shine my light—he was always there lurking in the shadows. Every cell of my body was geared to safeguard and defend all that was so precious to me.

But here was the gold in the dark. I kept asking, *Why has this experience shown up? What is it here to teach me? What am I to learn from this? How does this serve me?* In time, my understanding came into focus.

Greek and Latin roots of the word "hero" mean "defender" and "protector." In order to build a strong case that would get the FBI involved and give them something to work with, I had to summon all of my masculine energy. I had to call in my great protector. I had to be the hero at every turn to confront this threat on a daily basis for years. I had to see this through and make sure my family was safe—safe not only from physical harm but from the deep-seated darkness of a criminal mind who had turned his obsession into emotional terrorism for my family, using the internet as his weapon to weave his web of assaults on me and my daughters daily in one hundred different ways.

I don't necessarily believe that everything happens for a reason. But our minds must find the reason why things happen—and my natural sense of optimism wants to make sense of things. My deepest desire is to personally grow and widen my understanding of this spiritual-human adventure we are on. When you can be brave and courageous while dealing with unthinkable adversity and use the circumstances to reveal something profound about your growth, you have met the jagged edge. Courage requires true grit, that stuff inside that pushes you forward even when you want to fall down and crumble. It does not require the absence of anger. Sometimes anger serves us well because it fuels the fire of change. It gives us strength to stand and fight where flight simply isn't an option. It's truly OK to feel your anger and allow it to catalyze you into right action.

There were those who said to me, "Shhhhh . . . you don't want to give him attention because it fuels him." To that I said, *"Bullshit."* The dragon had breathed fire upon us, penetrating our lives without consent. Keeping quiet at any point did not change his obsession or the disease that fueled him. More than empowering (although it was that, too), it was a life-changing decision to stand up and, through my actions and words, say, *No. I will not be a victim. I will be anything but quiet. I will document every detail I can. I will shine the light of truth on this crime. And I will see that justice is done.* International cyber-harassment crimes affect many people around the world. I wanted laws to protect against this twenty-first-century reality, and now, thankfully, we have them.

Something else that came into focus for me during this time was the callous mistreatment of widows and widowers. People think we are weak—but I want people to know that surviving spouses are among the toughest birds there are! The more this stalker tormented me online, the more he threatened us, the more I reared up as the warrior. I remember the moment he called my home phone and I answered, not knowing it would be him. I recognized his accent immediately. As he began his litany of threats, I screamed, "You will stop! You will not bring harm on us any longer. You will go to jail for this when the laws catch up to you!" I put my stake in the ground. It took years of tenacity and daily help from my assistant at the time. We collected files of thousands of his delusional tweets and postings and threats against all that I loved and held dear to me. Seven years later he was tried in an English court and found guilty.

In the name of the divine, my anger and anguish have served me well, and I am grateful to have had the strength to see this situation through. I believe that I am wired to grow into my heroic self rather than wither into victimhood. I believe we all are. In his book *Upside: The New Science of Post-Traumatic Growth,* Jim Rendon eloquently writes about how the emotional and physical pain caused by traumatic events can become a force for dramatic change, moving us to find the deeper meaning of our lives. (The term "post-traumatic growth" was coined in the 1990s by Richard Tedeschi and Lawrence Calhoun of the University of North Carolina.) Like me, Rendon views traumatic events as times of passage through darkness that are a part of our shared archetypal story of the return to wholeness. Remembering that there is a purpose for these experiences has been a balm to my soul as my daughters and I continue to heal from that chapter of our lives.

On retreat in Hawaii to write this book, I'm reflecting on what it would have been like to be those first islanders to discover what we call the Hawaiian Islands. Heartbreak of some kind drives people away from their homeland to explore the unknown and to put their stake in the ground of new territory to call *home.* Nature also wages war on Mother Earth with volcanoes, tsunamis, forest fires, and storms to bring change to her. We can derive strength from our ancestors and from looking to nature to give us the hope and courage we need to proceed forward. No matter what heartbreak you face brought on by life-altering circumstances, here's where you will solidify your commitment to being the hero of your story. Here is where you will find the open door to something unknown and the courage to step in. Here's where you will put your stake in the ground with a hard stand of commitment to the new territory that will be your new home.

THE STARR PATH OF GROWTH

Personal growth happens because you choose to open to it. You can choose growth independent of suffering, but suffering has a way of bringing you to yourself and the truth like nothing else. There is a vast world of self-discovery where the paradox is that you find your connection to humanity as you learn about yourself. When you explore your true nature, you have the opportunity to fall in love with what you find—like eating an artichoke one petal at a time until you get to the yummy, soft, and succulent heart. We are far more alike than we are different, and the more we know ourselves, the greater connection we feel to others. The more we love ourselves, the more we are capable of loving others. As we dive deep for the pearl of wisdom, so is our understanding and compassion accessed through consciousness and awareness of the meaning of life, and we experience the joy of pursuing our human potential.

Growth is not linear but rather chaotic at best. It is simultaneously a "three steps forward, three steps back," and "two steps to the left and one to the right" process. Many attempt to make it a linear, step-by-step process, but these steps can only present a framework or structure to inspire you in the mess of your own inner journey. And within all of it—all of the confusion and clarity, the pain and wonder—there can be a fluidity of grace that carries you. You probably know from your own hard-won experience that growth is less like a romantic waltz and more like the style of dance known as contact improv, where the uprisings of your lessons can get a bit wild and sweaty. The spontaneous and sometimes disorienting movements of your growth process ask you to surrender and trust—surrender to the fact that your life has changed, trust your divinely guided instincts while walking on unknown terrain, and trust your ability to find the emotional truth of your circumstance or situation. This part of your journey is about trusting that as you embrace life as it is, invoking grace to accompany you and allowing yourself to expand and develop on your own, knowing that in time you will understand why your soul has called this in for your growth—even if it's messy.

Things happen, and we find the reason why, and this is a very important distinction. Herein lies the greatest edge of your growth; it is in this understanding and in this process of allowance and finding the lessons in all things, good and bad. My good friend Karen Salmansohn calls it the "blesson" (the blessing in the lesson).

One of the most important early teachers in my life taught a mantra that became a life practice to me and to Richard. It's what I have called the STARR path of growth: *Surrender, Trust, Accept—Release, Receive.* I had no idea earlier in my life just how important it would become. In our youth, it worked pretty well in traffic, and as it turns out, it also works in grief. It's an amazing tool for helping you make choices at this point. This is another profoundly important moment on the road of your journey when you are being asked to surrender to and trust "what is" and integrate what may feel impossible to you right now as you accept your current situation. You may not be in the happiest segment of your life story, but you will soon realize that there is a new beginning happening in this ending. As you seek to understand what this situation or obstacle is here to teach you about yourself and embrace this process of transformation, you will be on your way back to a life of joy. The STARR mantra allows you to heal, grow, and transform—and prevents you from getting stuck as a victim who stays bitter, shut down, stagnant, and unwilling to change. As a path of growth, the practice is divided into two main phases, which

I'll guide you through in the Soul Inquiry process at the end of the chapter.

In the first phase, as you surrender your preconceived notions and thoughts about how you think this experience should be, trust your heart, trust in the divine spirit and the people around you, and accept that your situation is what it is. The idea of surrendering control can be so daunting because we live under the illusion that we have control over our life plans. To paraphrase Joseph Campbell, we must be willing to let go of the life we've planned, so as to have the life that is waiting for us. The act of surrender and trust is a portal that opens you to grace and the myriad possibilities that exist, and the universe begins to conspire on your behalf with unlimited momentum to bring the best plan of action to your attention at the right time.

When Lisa was going through cancer, she surrendered to the treatments, she surrendered to the quiet and stillness necessary after each treatment, she chose to trust the plan that her doctors had for her, and, yes, she accepted that this was in fact her healing journey to undertake. She couldn't wish it away. Surrender, trust, and acceptance of what was happening—in her body, mind, and spirit—were pivotal in Lisa's healing. She did not surrender the fight for her life but rather came to a deep emotional place where she could allow her body to kick into healing. She let go of worrying and leaned into fear. She came to understand at this point, as many people discover in the depths of a serious illness, that it wasn't that she was going to learn how to die, but that she was going to learn how to live.

You enter phase two as you accept your circumstances and release your fears to receive the blessings and wisdom, your holy grail, which will help keep you moving forward. As part of our early morning ritual, Richard and I would meditate together and repeat this prayer: "Divine love, play me as an instrument in your finely tuned orchestra of life." I still say this prayer today. By asking to be an instrument or a vehicle, I surrender my ego to divine love. Letting go of my problems to divine guidance makes life feel far easier. When I can release my worries and stress, I return to the moment where life is happening now. And in this moment, all is well.

When I bump up against a problem that nags at me—as I did countless times when I was dealing with the stalker—there is one question I ask myself: *Can I change this situation?* If the answer is *Not at the moment*, then I surrender and pray.

To ask is to open the door to receive. It takes a certain amount of humility to acknowledge that we don't have all of the answers to our questions and concerns. The power of any request or prayer is truly in the act of asking and of surrendering. Practicing "let go, let God" helps you get out of your own way and shift your whole way of being from stress and worry into more peace and serenity in the present moment. This process of asking is also like fishing. You cast out your line (your concern, worry, or intent), trusting that it will land in the right place at the right time. As you release it to the sea, you simply gather your bearings and wait. As you release your troubles into divine love through prayer or meditation, the pressure is off of you for now. You have let it go to something beyond, and rest assured, the universe has your back.

The answers will surely come, like the line that's been cast, because you have let go and are open to receiving guidance—guidance that will come in the way that you need it. It may come in the form of a new opportunity, a piece of useful information, a referral to an amazing support person, a connection to a friend's network, or any number of small or large miracles. And it's really OK not to know sometimes;

you'll know when you know. (That's trusting and allowing life to reveal itself to you.) It's all perfect as it is.

To completely let go is to be free of attachment. This, like most things, is easier said than done. I can clearly see when I'm attached to a set of circumstances or a specific outcome, because it causes me internal discord. I can alleviate much of my suffering and angst by examining my preferences and expectations and seeing which ones to drop. Once I let go, I feel more inner peace, and it's far easier to access my inner wisdom.

As I learned through the crucible of losing my husband, at some point in our lives there comes a request from the deepest well of our being to let go for purposes that lie beyond our normal daily awareness. We let go to receive the gift of change that will be the wisdom and clarity gained so that we live better than we have ever lived before.

HOLD ON . . . HOLD ON

One day the Queen of Death fiercely blew open my door, the mirror of my beloved gone. She came to me, and I was raw, vulnerable, feeling like an abandoned child with arms stretched upward, flailing like a fish out of water. She removed my mask, and together we viewed my shattered heart. Then she spoke these words:

Follow me.

In time, you will be whole again. But first . . .

It is your turn to dive deep into the abyss. Dive into the darkness, black as night, and keep going. Be not afraid, for I will go there with you. And remember, darkness is only the absence of light. Tumble and get munched by the waves of sorrow as they are

cleansing you with the release of your tears and screams and
expression. What you will discover is an incredible gift: what it
means to truly live.

Each of us, in transition, will eventually embrace with open
arms a new life. In order to really live, you must make peace with
the shadow of death. But first, you must go through a process of
ordination to release and let go of your attachments. Like strings
and cords that hold and restrain you, they bind you to an identity
masquerading as yourself. This process will chop them to ribbons.

I know you thought life was one way and now you feel isolated,
in pain, and alone . . . but I am here to usher you home.

Grace be with you.

In the years following this loving confrontation with the divine
feminine, I have increasingly noticed the play of the archetypes of
the masculine and feminine that live inside all of us. Deep in our
DNA we are inextricably bound to these collective energetic patterns
that have formed from thousands of years of language and story
being handed down through the ages. We cannot deny the wisdom that
comes through this innate mythical understanding that surfaces in
our being when we need only a thread of light amidst the darkness.

With this light, I began to see how the situation with the stalker
was playing on a grander scale the persecution of the masculine over
the feminine. He had targeted us as three women without a man in
the house to defend us. He, like many, preyed on what is defined by the
chauvinistic mindset as "weak without a man."

Yet the feminine can be fierce warriors, too, and certainly the
stalker had ignited that spark in me that grew into a feminine fire-
wall. He had ignited all of the archetypes that lay dormant beneath
twenty-five years of protection by a gentle but powerful warrior man.
The stalker became the catalyst—the dragon to be conquered, the

obstacle that would reveal the depth and breadth of my strength, courage, and commitment to the path.

But first, I had to live the mantra and follow it like a lighted path through the darkness:

I surrender, trust, and accept . . .
I release . . . I receive . . .

It is in surrender that she, *Grace,* will come to you. It is in the annihilation of your former life and identity that you will be reborn. It is in the ending that the beginning of your hero's journey is spawned. Your journey into the unknown, brought through loss of some kind, will remove the shackles of your suffering, and you will emerge anew.

Physical death brings us through a portal into pure consciousness, whether you are the one to shed your body like a well-worn pair of shoes, or you remain planted in life on the earth to grieve. Both souls experience an annihilation that is liberating. Richard's death breathed new life into me as my wisdom blossomed like the lotus from the impossibly murky waters. Thousands of years flew by as I traveled into the darkness, in surrender, trusting in love to lead the way, and accepting and releasing the illusion of control, leaving the mask of the ego where my broken heart lay in pieces. Shattered, with my broken heart mending, in the expansion I receive a new life.

I surrender
I trust
I accept
I release
I receive
The northern STARR that leads me home in stormy seas . . .
I adjust, I refine, I live.

Now it's your turn to see how the five-pointed STARR mantra can support your process of learning, understanding, and healing at the jagged edge of your journey. But first, remember where you are on your journey toward wholeness. You cannot see the future yet, and that is as it should be. It's essential that you take the time to recover from your loss.

I will remind you, just as I was reminded, to hold on.

In time, you're going to see everything you need to see. And something great—something worthy of a queen or a king—will come out of this formidable experience that life has brought to your door.

> **SOUL MANTRA:**
>
> Gently close your eyes and breathe golden light into your lungs, your belly, and down into your toes. Then repeat the mantra:
>
> *I surrender, trust, release, and receive.*
> *I surrender, I receive.*

THE SOUL INQUIRY:
LESSONS FROM THE JAGGED EDGE OF GROWTH

PART 1—*The Lessons*

You are standing on very fertile ground right now, and I want you to maximize this time period for the profound growth opportunity that it is. Your heart, mind, and body are resilient and becoming more so all the time. I ask that you make the most of this expanded Soul Inquiry and writing process, bringing out into the light everything you're thinking and feeling about where you are in your life right now.

Without overthinking any of the questions, write down the first uncensored answers that come to you. Some of the questions are similar, but I ask that you trust the slight variations in wording for how they may reveal specific pieces of your unique story and the gifts contained therein.

1. What is your greatest obstacle (or obstacles) at this point of your journey? What is your "dragon" on the path toward wholeness?

2. Why has this obstacle shown up for you?

3. How do you see this situation, circumstance, or issue as a key life lesson?

4. How are your experiences at the jagged edge of your life serving you right now?

5. Tapping into your wildest dreams, how could you allow this obstacle to expand you? How could it add to your life?

6. Are you committed to your growth? Be specific here. How much time will you spend each day working on your inner growth—reflecting, contemplating, processing?

PART 2—*The STARR Mantra: A Process of Letting Go to Receive*

As we've been exploring, most of the time, growth happens along a nonlinear and circuitous path. Transformation has a timeless and untamable quality. Paradoxically, using healing tools and personal development processes in a step-by-step way can bring tremendous clarity, giving the mind comfort—as well as sparking those rushes of insight and excitement that help to put the wind back in your sails. I believe that you will find this mantra helpful in all areas of life. Therefore, now is the perfect time to apply the STARR mantra to your healing journey—to Surrender, Trust, and Accept; to Release and Receive.

Phase 1—Surrender, Trust, and Accept

The focus here is on surrendering preconceived notions about how this experience or situation should be, allowing your body to reveal information to you about your feelings, trusting your heart, trusting

the divine, trusting your intuition, and accepting that this obstacle—
this jagged-edge lesson—has found its way to your door.

To help you in this process, please journal and answer these questions:

1. What do you believe about this challenge or obstacle
    that is having a negative impact on you? What are the
    limiting beliefs of the story that you tell yourself?
2. Are you willing to surrender that belief, idea, or story?
3. Who or what do you most need to trust right now?
4. What is your body informing you to do?
5. Can you allow your feelings to surface? What are those
    feelings?
6. What do you need to accept that has been difficult to face
    and embrace?

Phase 2—Release and Receive

The focus is on letting go, releasing your fears, and readying yourself
to receive the blessings and wisdom, and to receive the joy of letting
go and opening to something new. The willingness to release and receive in this way will not only help you to keep moving forward but
will also help you to fully emerge into your new life.

To help you in this process of letting go, please journal and answer these questions:

1. What are you most afraid of in this situation or
    circumstance that has placed you at the jagged edge?
2. What would help you to release the fear? Is it an
    action step? Are there words you need to hear? Is there

something that you need to express to someone in your life?

3. What feelings are present?

4. How can you allow your feelings to be expressed and released?

5. What wisdom do you now hold in your heart because of this challenge, this experience? What is the blessing that it has come to lay at your feet?

Your New Story • *transformational writing process*

Articulate your jagged edge of growth. Bringing together the rich gems of insight and understanding that you've excavated in the Soul Inquiry above, write in narrative form about this stage of your healing process. You are facing down your dragon (or perhaps multiple dragons/obstacles). Your willingness to surrender, trust, accept, release, and receive its gifts is a testament to the power of your heart. This is where you begin to transform your story forever into the hero's journey. This is where you rise above the gravitational pull of your pain.

_____

_____

_____

_____

_____

_____

Chapter 5

Discovery, Recovery, and Rediscovery

> **The Promise of Chapter 5**—At this stage, you are aware that you are not the same. While there is heartbreak, there is also an opportunity to rediscover your true Self and reclaim the passions that you've left behind to live the life you've lived.

When Richard died, I quickly went from an envied woman to a woman who was pitied. In the blink of an eye, I changed costumes from devoted wife and strong dutiful mother to single mother, bereft and besieged by self-doubt and fears that I might not be able to manage my responsibilities on my own.

Maybe you can relate intimately to my abrupt transformation. Whoever and whatever you thought you were before, you are now *something else*. This is the point in your journey when you must confront a loss of identity that has come through an ego annihilation. You have experienced the death of a life—yours has changed so much that it feels like parts of you have died, leaving you with uncertainty about who you are. Yes, it's a radical change that sets so many fine adjustments in motion. Like an earthquake, the ground beneath your feet has shifted, and it *feels* different now. How could it not? You are birthing a new identity; moreover, you are feeling exposed and vulnerable. This time period comes with a host of big questions, including how to be with other people, in all the ordinary social ways, and how to proceed forward in this new life.

These are not only issues you struggle with in your own mind while you wrestle with this uneasy feeling of having your identity in crisis. They are issues you will face when you are among your people, even those who are supportive, because of all the ways your community, friends, and family see and respond to your new identity, too. I was a woman in my forties with a family, and most of my closest friends were also married with families. This was our community, and we were fully immersed in a world where it was normal to be in a partnered relationship. And—let's face it—whether you are divorced or widowed in this family-oriented culture, there is a real (if usually unspoken) stigma about being single. Of course, none of them blamed me for being widowed, and now single, but I couldn't help feeling like it was harder for us to relate to each other when their whole concept of me had been defined by my marriage and family life. They needed some time to adjust, too. In turn, their view of me contributed greatly to my own feelings of who I was in the world. Suddenly, an awkwardness exists, as everyone adjusts to this new identity you have until you make your way into this new life. Some will embrace it with you, while others won't be able to. If you have lost your partner, your new single status, to some, may represent a threat—and to others, may be a reminder of something that they just can't live with on a day-to-day basis. They are very aware that this could, after all, happen to them. As is often the case, your true friends will be revealed; they come to your side and stay steady for the long haul. Your angels show up.

Everyone on the journey from heartbreak to wholeness faces this same challenge, and everyone questions: *Who am I?* The poignant nuances of this question arise from the depths of your own particular heartbreak.

Who am I alone?

Who am I without my beloved?

Who am I as a single person?

Who am I as a solo parent?

Who am I without the body I used to know, when I was healthy?

Who am I without the respect that came with my job?

Who am I without the financial standing I had?

Who am I now that I'm no longer young?

Who am I since I took refuge in a country that isn't my own?

Who am I after the traumatic event that changed me?

Who am I now . . . after all of this has happened?

Our suffering leads us into deeper corridors of ourselves than we could have imagined before. What we discover in heartbreak often extends beyond the relationship—or the home or the job or the way of life—that has now irrevocably changed. *We discover that there are aspects of ourselves that we have left behind in order to live the life we have lived.*

Let's go on a reconnaissance mission together to find and retrieve the real you—the essential you that existed, that has always been present even if subdued, and that always will be, before, during, and after everything that happens in the epic adventure of your life.

DISCOVERY—THE POWER OF BELIEFS

Our beliefs are one of the most powerful tools with which we shape our identity. What you believe to be true opens or closes you to a myriad of possibilities. Much of what you believe may be buried deep in your unconscious mind and is only visible to you as you remove the filter through which you view what you see in the world. No matter how close you are to someone, no two people view the world exactly alike; we view the world through our own unique lens, built from every experience we have and every ideal that we connect to. The latest research on happiness, as seen in Shawn Achor's book *Before Happiness,* shows that we are exposed to 11 million bits of information every second, but our minds only process 40 pieces per second. That doesn't change the fact that there are still 11 million possibilities present, but our deeply ingrained beliefs about everything make us choose what we will expose ourselves to every second. The quality of our beliefs is so vital to how we experience life that I have come to differentiate and define ego and unhealthy ego based on that. We all have our ego-designed self. I use a small *s* here to define that identity as either overly grand or small-minded, narrow, and limiting—which is how ego defines *us.* But we also have our true Self—that which we are born with and who we truly are from our soul. Just as our body has its genetic DNA structure, so too does our soul come with a blueprint—the master plan for discovering, knowing, and expressing the greater Self's potential through pursuing a life of meaning. The unhealthy ego, on the other hand, lives by a tightly edited script about what's OK and what isn't—who we get to be and what we get to do. It's the limiting beliefs and stories we tell about who we are that build a fortress around the heart—one block at a time—cutting us off from experiencing ourselves and allowing others to see who we *really* are.

We literally shape our brains and neuro-pathways based on our repeated thoughts. As Dr. Shauna Shapiro writes, "What you practice grows stronger." This is why it's so important to consciously choose thoughts that lift you up and widen your world.

What I want you to know is that this is a moment-to-moment practice of being awake. While it's simple to write about, it takes practice and choosing all day long to be present. I have mastered this much of the time, but I still struggle because the mind is like a monkey that jumps wildly with reckless abandon. As you adopt a form of meditation practice where you can quiet your mind, you will find it easier to practice training your mind to access your mental health and well-being. As you come into your body, completely present, notice how you awaken with a feeling of peace and awe. From this place that you land in you, in your body, mindful of your feelings—this is where your true nature rings loud and clear.

RECOVERY OF THE SELF—GATHERING UP THE PIECES

In the aftermath of your heartbreak, are you seeing how certain thoughts and beliefs have limited you? Have you believed that the marriage, the relationship, the family, the career, the education, or the reputation you nurtured came with specific requirements? You may have believed that some of who you are fit well within the parameters of these roles, and some did not. For example, you may have deferred your choice to be independent to a not-so-healthy codependent relationship, leaving you feeling incomplete without the person who has died or left. A friend of mine, Alan, described feeling like he lay in dismembered parts all over the floor during the heartbreak of his divorce. But it wasn't only the parts that got shredded in the breakup that he was feeling the loss of. Being extremely independent and something of an epicurean by nature, he also became aware of parts of himself that he had suppressed throughout much of his nine-year marriage. For example, he came to realize that he had covered up a great deal of his enthusiasm and intensity to live in a partnership that wasn't completely aligned with his true nature.

The acute awareness that you have lost something of your true nature to live the life you are now grieving marks a turning point, not only in your process of healing but in your hero's journey toward wholeness. This is the point where you can recover and rediscover those aspects of your Self that you have denied expression to, leaving you wounded, incomplete, suffering, and out of touch with your essence. I want you to realize that these parts have always been there; they have just been left unattended in a backroom, dormant for a time. Now you can make the choice to acknowledge those areas that have atrophied from lack of use and pick up the pieces. You can dismantle limiting and false beliefs so you don't get stuck in your old habits and your suffering ways that have led you astray. This is the point in your journey where suffering becomes optional, and the pivot happens when you release yourself from the trance of believing that your fulfillment will come from the outside. Our culture operates with a collective belief that we will be happy when something happens that we desire on the outside or when some other person loves us. Song lyrics, storybooks, movies, family lineage, and other reflectors of our shared beliefs about relationships say, "You will be completed by another." These deep-seated ideas perpetuate a myth brought on by the collective egocentric belief that we are not whole within ourselves.

The absolute truth is **You were born complete.** You were born with a human design that is primed and ready to blossom into the fullness of *you*—like the acorn that holds the astounding pattern within it that becomes the oak tree. Before adding anything or anyone to the mix of your life, you are already complete on your own. You've just temporarily forgotten who you are.

Ancient philosophers and sages have long attempted to remind us of our innate wholeness. Hermeticism, the ancient Greek philosophical tradition based on the idea of "As above, so below; As within, so without," played a key role in the early development of science and the theory that "the part" (the microcosm) always reflects "the whole" (the macrocosm)—and vice versa. The Emerald Tablet of the Hermetic tradition poetically describes how opposites come together in their dance "to accomplish the miracle of the One Thing." You are that miracle—right now, just as you are. At the heart of the hero's journey is the return to this knowing and its immanent joy.

Whatever you have lost or whatever you feel is missing on the outside plays a crucial role in healing what feels broken inside. Truth is, we are as we are from the inside out, and our life circumstances reveal what lies deep inside our minds. Life shows us the places within that need our loving attention—the aspects of ourselves that we have neglected or forgotten. It is our soul-work to nurture and recover these parts and to remember who we are, unbounded to how we define ourselves. Another universal law—the law of resonance—says like attracts like. This means that if you are feeling broken, it's likely that you may attract someone else who feels broken, and if you are feeling your wholeness, you will possibly attract another person who also feels whole. When we can take a step back and look at our relationships and interactions with a neutral eye, they will lead us directly to the places within us that need our focus and care.

Let's peer into and magnify for a moment what relationship is. Intimacy is about looking into someone and seeing them from the inside out—seeing their heart and depth, beyond their physical presence. But as we peer into their eyes to see their soul, what is reflected back is our own image. As we see them, the closer we are to the other, the more we are actually able to see ourselves. It's as if our thoughts, feelings, and beliefs are reflected back to us through our interactions with others—especially our romantic partners. For the past two decades, neuroscientists have been researching the biological basis for this phenomenon in the study of mirror neurons. Mirror neurons, seen by many in the scientific community as a cornerstone of human empathy, allow us to observe something in another human being—he recoils from touching a hot stove, or she's crying in sadness, for example—and feel it as if it were happening to us. Of course, our felt experiences in relationships can swing wildly, moving from feelings of tenderness and bliss to aggravation and disconnection. For example, have you noticed that in an argument, anger can serve to feed the fire between you—until it's hard to remember who got angry first? That is the mirror. When you observe another, your brain thinks it's happening to you.

But, understanding this, the converse is also true. If you are grounded in the wholeness of who you are, strongly rooted in your mental and emotional well-being and health, you will be better equipped to maintain a position of love amidst anger or chaos. This would be your intention, your baseline for connecting. When you are able to access your internal CEO, the prefrontal cortex of your brain, during an emotional engagement of any kind, then you can bring a calm resolve to stay centered. As you do this by taking deep breaths, and being mindful of how you are feeling, you can be open and listen from your heart to the *feelings* stirred by the interaction. And you can stand as the mirror of unconditional love. As my marriage ripened, I realized that if I was feeling taken for granted in our relationship, Richard was likely feeling that way, too. Sharpening my own gratitude became a strategy to become the mirror, and then offering him some kind words of appreciation always helped to window-clean our temporarily fogged-up feelings and brighten the lens through which we viewed our day-to-day interactions. It's really true that a little gratitude goes a long way and lets us become a wonderful reflection to each other.

I remember a specific moment of frustration that Richard was having during an extremely chaotic time in our lives. After the kids went to school one day, we had a heart-to-heart discussion. It was unusual for Richard to be frustrated, but this time he was pointing out, as if he held an invisible scorecard, all the things he did versus those I did in our household. At first, I was annoyed with him, as anyone would be. But then something clicked in me as I accessed my mental health and wholeness. I was able to listen to his feelings and not to the content he was delivering. My relationship was suddenly far more important to me than being right in this argument. The truth in this moment was that he didn't feel appreciated. (I felt exactly the same way, but his feelings were more important to me at this time.) There we sat, in our big house at our kids' small table, having one of the few arguments we ever had and a discussion that healed something for Richard. We suddenly looked at each other sitting at the little table and broke out into laughter at the absurdity of where we had landed—so symbolic of the smallness of the ego mind, the train of thoughts we can climb aboard that tells us something is lacking, that makes us point fingers and keep score. Landing in the smallest, most emotionally confining place with the fewest satisfying options, there is nowhere to go but to return to our heart—our Home in Love.

As we begin to understand the power of this mirror, we can now clearly see that what we are temporarily missing, even longing for, is the intimacy that we shared in that relationship that is no longer. Knowing this, it's easy to understand why this time period hurts so much—and that what has fallen away is a reflection of what we must rediscover within ourselves.

The light inside the darkness of this time is the opportunity to look deeper within and rekindle and strengthen the relationship you have with spirit, the source of life and inspiration. To fall in love with life is the same as becoming a mirror reflection of all that is divine in this universe—that beauty that reflects back to you in all the masculine and feminine qualities integrated in perfect union. While your relationship has ended, your life can now become your mirror.

WHAT ABOUT LOVE? WHAT RELATIONSHIP BEST SERVES ME *NOW*?

Picking ourselves up and piecing together a new sense of self, we eventually find ourselves reaching toward relationship again, in one way or another—either with someone new or the partner who has weathered the crisis alongside us. In either case, we often have to confront some unresolved heartache that remains as an obstacle to connection.

A friend of mine, Sahar, a beautiful woman who grew up in Tehran and migrated to the United States with her family thirty years ago, has been married to her Iranian husband, Hassan, for the past twenty-eight years. She came over at sixteen years of age wearing a black veil and the standard Muslim dress, but since then her life has become very American. It was a real shock one day, though, when she looked in Hassan's phone for a number and saw a text message that read, "I'm so excited to see you before your long travels away." With a bit more searching, she realized that Hassan had been flirting with a woman who worked at the health club where he had a membership and might have gone even further into an extramarital affair. Brokenhearted, she did not leave Hassan, because they were still raising their youngest daughter, and she simply wasn't sure whether he had actually cheated. It didn't matter much, because their trust was broken, as were his vows to her. As she dealt with her anger, she retreated inward. I watched her begin her journey to recover those parts of herself that she had left lying like a doormat in her more than subservient marriage. That year, she did so many things she had always wanted to do, things that were expressions of her inner beauty. She birthed a jewelry business where she spent hours beading and creating gorgeous things (all of which I wanted!). She recovered her inner healer and became a Reiki Master and Kundalini yoga instructor. Her meditation practice flourished and brought her a quiet peace that allowed her to eventually forgive and let go and begin anew in her marriage. It was her broken heart that told her it was time for her to own her own life, and she intuitively went on a quest to find strength as she recovered her passions, gathering up those aspects that would develop her and create the opportunity to heal. Sahar created a life that was independent and codependent no more, and her marriage is not the same; now, it is better.

I was speaking with a friend the other day, and he commented that he didn't feel worthy of love. At the heart of our unhealthy ego is the fear that somehow we are not good enough as we are. Truth is, many people feel this way, and it's easy to adopt a lifestyle of routine and structure to avoid being hurt—to avoid true intimacy. I can see this sometimes in my own single-woman lifestyle that revolves around staying busy: too busy to truly fall in love with another partner—too busy to be hurt. When this happens, my ego has been effective at telling me that I must create safety in isolation.

The unhealthy ego may be subdued for a time, but when wounded and scared, it is triggered, and one of the ways it creeps back up is through negative judgmental self-talk that separates us from ourselves and others. Self-judgment is often at the root of negative self-talk.

Silently, in an internal battle, we say things to ourselves that we would never say to a friend: *You're not enough for him/her. You're damaged goods. You should have known better. When will you get it together? You can't be trusted on your own. You're hopeless in those situations.*

We all do this negative self-talk, beating ourselves up every day in a variety of ways, but it doesn't serve us well. In fact, it's what exhausts us and holds us back. We may mistakenly think that our negative self-talk is motivating us to do better, but it's really only making us feel shitty about ourselves. For example, you may look in the mirror and notice some aspect of your appearance that you are not happy with, and for those few seconds be speaking negatively to yourself. Rather, you could look in the mirror and simply notice yourself gently and compassionately—without the negative monologue.

The same is true for judging your healing process and thinking you "should" be doing it better, faster, or differently. Instead, lovingly notice your healing process. What's happening with it? Where could you use some encouragement? What's showing signs of change? We need to celebrate moving—only moving, albeit in baby steps. When you judge where you are in your healing process, and compare it to where you want to be, you create a mountain to climb when all you need to do is take small steps daily on a well-laid path through the valley, keeping the mountain in the long view to call you forward.

In the wake of heartbreak, the right time to begin even the most tentative steps back into exploring new connections, and possibly dating or being open to a healing companion, is different for everyone. For me, it was helpful in this stage to have a male perspective. In those early days of grief when I felt so desperate and in need of a male point of view, I met a man who had been a colleague and friend of

Richard's. We struck up a long-distance email correspondence that eventually blossomed into a short romance and what I believe will be a lifelong friendship. When I was grieving Richard's loss, this man was going through a breakup as well, and I appreciated his thoughts and companionship. Our conversations really helped me along my journey, because he was truly wise and traversing his own feelings of heartbreak. As we met in person after months of communication, we forged a strong connection that took a turn toward being a "friends with benefits" open relationship, which was new to me, and extremely different from my life as a married woman. This newfound sexuality, plus the concept of having love and companionship without commitment, was somehow freeing and certainly all that I needed or wanted during these early stages of survival. But it was also confusing. And yet, in that confusion, I realized that I was going to have to resist the temptation to fall into patterns I already knew were outdated for me at this juncture, as I stood as a single widowed woman who was trying on new roles in every aspect of my life. I knew that I was not at all ready for a steady committed relationship, and the long distance between our countries proved to be a perfect design for keeping a commitment at bay in this healing friendship.

I bumped into Briana while out shopping. Briana was in her midtwenties, a college graduate, and she shared that she and her boyfriend of four years had broken up. She said, "I was blinded by my trusting nature to his cheating. Even after I caught him the first time, I stayed, believing he would change as he had promised to and love me more. I don't even know how many times he went out on me after that, but now I'm left asking myself, how is it that my self-worth is so low that I would stay with a guy like that for so long?" Briana continued sharing how she was intentionally not dating or going out, for a time, because she wanted to know who she was outside of a relationship. She chose to step onto a path of self-discovery and spent the last year recovering who she was before the relationship in a quest to discover her independent nature—and to learn the art of discernment. In time, the wisdom of her recovery will be reflected in her outer world. The self-loving act of embracing the many parts of herself will allow Briana to find a man worthy of her attributes.

And then there was Carrie. Carrie had lost her husband in a train accident and found her way to one of my Heartbroken Open grief circles shortly after. In a chance meeting months later, she looked remarkably light and glowing—notably shining much brighter than in those early grief days. Carrie leaned in, cupping her hand for secrecy, and whispered to me, "I followed your advice, Kris." Wondering what I had told her, I replied a bit in jest, "Oh, what's that—dare I ask?" She had taken on a healing companion—her own version of a "friends with benefits" relationship. You see, when you feel like you're going to die, and especially if this is something that you fear, a healing companion who is a safe haven can really help you choose to live. Sexual energy is a very alive physical expression, and as long as you don't make the relationship mean something more than it is, it can be a potent healing force in this transitional time.

Please keep in mind that you are vulnerable right now, and it's important to choose wisely and not from the fear of being alone. A big question for many in this stage is: What kind of relationship is the right kind right now? How does love fit into *this* life? If your initiation came in the form of the loss of your partner, this is not yet the time to be deeply connecting with other people in a quest for life partnership. What this part of the journey shows you is how to forge a new relationship with love by building a new relationship with yourself first.

In our minds, it's easy to fall in love when we're not in a committed relationship and have some distance from the actual experience that real relationship stuff is made of—the day-to-day interactions and habits. It's easy to romanticize when we're longing for another. One of my relationships over this time taught me that I could fall in love with the potential of the relationship rather than what it actually was. And I spent a number of years tied up in a dream state of "what could be, if only." One of the most transformative ways you can approach this time is to look deeply at your past relationships. What worked for you and what didn't? If there were important relationships that came to an end through a breakup or divorce, be honest with yourself about why they didn't work out. Take inventory with as much realness and courage as you can muster. As you begin to get emotionally present with yourself—with what really works for you at this point in your life— the way forward will become clearer. I got very clear during this part of my journey that it wouldn't work for me to ever be a traditional wife again. Despite what a wonderful marriage I had, I discovered that I had given up too much of myself to my role. I gave up personal dreams to be a wife and mother. As right as that was for me at that time, I wouldn't choose it now. I remembered why I'm here and am pursuing a life of service that has come through my journey with a message to deliver. And I can hold that paradox in my arms—my soul's path then was to be right where I was, and all of this loss and heartbreak happened to bring me to this place. I am different now.

This is the time to look back in order to move forward.

REDISCOVERY: RECLAIMING YOUR PASSION

I am one of those people who can honestly say that my life has been a personal growth odyssey of discovery, recovery, and rediscovery.

After I met my husband in college, we dived into the ephemeral together. We learned to meditate from a wonderful transpersonal therapist in Berkeley. We explored every healing modality that seemed useful, from cytotoxic food-allergy testing to Reichian breathwork to rebirthing. We were called by Sai Baba, who was a spiritual guru—a known avatar of our time, an embodiment of the divine. Although separated by oceans and continents and cultures, he became our teacher for many years as we magically built our lives together enveloped in the mystery.

That time of building also included recovery from an eating disorder that had begun when I was fourteen years old. By the time I reached twenty-four, I had learned that I was worthy of a whole life, and I didn't have to be perfect in it. It was ten years of learning and uncovering who I was at the root of my fears and inadequacies. Meeting my husband and being loved so unconditionally was a huge factor in my recovery. After many years of this deep dive into understanding my triggers of perfectionism and feelings of self-doubt, I began to unravel the habits and thoughts of fear that brought me to this dark place of turmoil and self-destruction—and was able to end the cycle of bingeing and purging. I embarked on a spiritual journey where I would realize it was my power to choose that would be my final step out.

One day as I sat in meditation, in my mind's eye I saw Sai Baba before me, sitting peacefully cross-legged in his orange robe and halo of hair, as he cupped his hands like a weight scale. With this image, I understood that each time I would overeat, it was my choice, and I could choose either way equally. I began to feel a new sense of internal power and control. A couple of years later, when I got pregnant with Jazz, it was my final healing, as I would not choose this for my daughter who was in my belly. It was realizing my power of choice that taught me at every meal that I could change my relationship to food and stop bingeing as a mechanism for relieving all the inner-world turmoil that was churning under the surface. And it was that "three steps forward and two steps back or to the side" nonlinear path that I walked for those ten years of healing that taught me that healing, whether from an addiction or heartbreak, is a step-by-step process and not always moving forward in a straight line.

Over the years, I found myself at the feet of many gurus—realizing upon my husband's death that there was no longer a reason to seek in another for what we are already connected to. The teachings of Sai Baba always pointed to this understanding, but it was easy to get caught up in all of the divine miracles that appeared to be coming through that being and not recognize them as a direct manifestation from my own beliefs and my openness to being in the flow of the mystery and the many possibilities that exist. In Richard's transition from form to formless, he had shown me that the divine source had become ever so clear to me—where I could meet and feel Richard now; where we are blissfully one. "Ride my wings of love," I would hear him say in my mind. And most important to me is that I found this place where I can continue my relationship with him while I am planted on the earth and he is in the realm of the divine. Like a string from my heart to the heavens, my husband's death has connected me more clearly with divine consciousness and, mostly, with a deep understanding that we are all but instruments of this tremendous source, having a spiritual experience while inhabiting a human body for a temporary bleep of a moment here.

But it was during an earlier period in my adult life, raising our children and living the American dream—a sleepwalking dream—

that I got caught up in it. For a time, I was lacking the drive to go inward and was more focused on my otherly outward world, lulled into a bit of complacency brought on by our success, when Norman Cousins's words rang loud and clear to me one morning:

The tragedy of life is not death but what we let die inside of us while we live.

It's very easy when you've had success to buy into the ego world of safety and the status quo of doing what everyone around you is doing, calling that "normal," and to drop into a habitual life of doing and staying busy, raising a family, buying a house and decorating it, and changing cars. But once you've chosen a spirit-driven path at any time in your life, you may go to sleep for a while; even the modern-day mystics do, but there's no going back. Spirit will speak—no matter what! I listened with deaf ears for a time, but spirit was whispering: *Something isn't right. You are not feeling passionate, and you don't even care. Your ego is ruling you, and you are allowing it to.*

Then the unthinkable happened that ordinary day, and I was shocked and cracked wide open and awake to all of it—especially to how asleep I had been. The contrast was undeniable.

Now I had a new and unusual relationship in my life, and my curiosity about the new feelings I was experiencing was piqued. While I was in pain, I was also feeling freer than I had ever felt. I somehow embraced a calm strength that resembled joy amidst sorrow. I could feel myself to be what I can now articulate as completely uncluttered by ego and extremely expressed, like my infant self before the mask of ego was created in my identity. I felt my true essence bubble up from that well that had been suppressed by ego, and as if a dam had broken, I felt authentically me in my truest essence. Jean Houston, the great harbinger of human potential, shows us that as we go back through our wounding and heal, we get to the heart of who we are at our essence. During these first months and years of grief, I was extremely present because the past held suffering, and looking forward held suffering, too. In the present vertically aligned moment, untethered to fear of the future or past regret, my ego stayed quiet, and I could settle into that feeling of being me. I had never felt more me, and I embraced this new feeling like a warm hug.

This is where my new identity would begin to form without holding on to "the perfect life." I would sit in the stillness, let go of the masks I had previously worn, and feel: *Oh*, this *is who I am*. This is where I began to recover and rediscover passion—the kind that would assist me in finding my purpose and living a purpose-driven life.

What you have lost opens you to discovery and recovery—to finding out something new and to *refinding* parts of who you are and what you love. What has been taken away in the present also gives you the opportunity to retrieve and revisit younger versions of yourself, parts of you that can come to your aid now as your heart is on the mend. There are interests that you felt passionate about that you may have left in the past in order to live the life you've lived. As an adult with real-world responsibilities, it may have become frivolous to think of yourself as an artist, sculptor, author, or musician. It's easy to get caught up in the roles we live. What activities or areas of interest are you naturally attracted to? What naturally comes up? Maybe you have loved nature so much—hiking and running and feeling the wind on your face—and yet somewhere along the line, you decided that "work must prevail" over these activities that feed your soul. Although being in the present offers its own kind of awakening, going back to what you've left behind is a medicine unlike any other.

While you are steeped in this part of the journey, where you are recovering so much of what matters to you, I invite you to answer the questions on the next page. Allow yourself the freedom to write down whatever spontaneously comes to mind.

REDISCOVERING YOUR PASSIONS

What are three things or experiences that bring you joy? (Even if you don't feel you have time to do them.)

_____

_____

_____

What are three things you loved to do as a child or a teen? (Hint: draw, play an instrument, sing in a choir, spend time in nature . . .)

_____

_____

_____

What are three ways you would like to serve others more? (For example, give more time to your family or community; give more money to charity . . .)

_____

_____

_____

In the days and weeks ahead, if you feel moved to add to your list of passions, do it! Let your joy flow. Also, the answers and clarity that come to you will feature greatly in the chapters ahead.

SOUL MANTRA:

Sit quietly and practice your soul mantra:

I love and respect myself fully and completely.
I am enough as I am.

THE SOUL INQUIRY:
WHAT CAN I DISCOVER, RECOVER, AND REDISCOVER NOW?

This Soul Inquiry marks a turning point in the journey: Whereas I have guided you through the inquiry processes so far, you are now ready for self-led inquiry. With each step you take to rediscover yourself, you are calling back your power.

1. What thoughts have become like sticky tape to make me suffer? And how do my sticky-tape thoughts make me feel?
2. What beliefs do I have that limit me and hold me back from healing?
3. How is my life a mirror to what I'm feeling?
4. In what part of my life have I been complacent or asleep?
5. What am I grateful for? (It can be one small thing.)
6. What kind of relationship best serves me now?

Your New Story • *transformational writing process*

Who are you now? Your new identity is forming, and your passions are becoming clear. Find a moment of stillness, to sense and feel who you are becoming, and write about who and what you are discovering.

_____

_____

_____

_____

_____

_____

_____

Chapter 6

Emerging Now

> **The Promise of Chapter 6**—You will discover what is emerging from you as you lean into your fears, access your courage, and step into the journey with both feet. You will answer the question "Who am I now?" Read on.

As I zipped my red dress closed, I was prepared to speak at the American Red Cross's Go Red for Women annual fund-raiser in February of 2014 in Sacramento. Arriving at the venue, at first I felt energized and eager to connect with this amazing audience, but I really did not feel like myself. I walked up to the podium but didn't feel grounded in my body as I looked out to the crowd. I felt as though my feet were elevated about three feet off the floor, and I was suspended in time. It was one of those dreaded moments on the platform as I delivered one of the worst speeches of my career. I couldn't wait to step down, and I had no idea why I was so distracted. I felt caught in a funnel of some kind—a whirlwind of energy. Moments later, as I took my seat, my phone vibrated. I could see it was the investigator who had finally taken interest in our stalking case. I excused myself as I accepted the international call from Wales. The chief investigator excitedly told me that they had arrested the stalker half an hour earlier—the same time I had taken the stage.

I suddenly realized why I felt elevated on the platform. It was because that dark energy was off of me for the first real time in seven years. I could feel the cord being cut, and I felt lifted out of my body. Our ordeal was now over. Simultaneously, I felt that a number of trying incidents were beginning to complete in my life. Situations that were difficult at best, and all happening concurrently with my grieving, were coming to a resolution. Now, I felt like a hang glider lifting off. I felt an energetic shift happening from what was previously like having fireworks of conflict constantly crackling overhead. This feeling was powerful and new; I was emerging into a brighter stage of my life and with new feelings of completion and peace; there was something emerging out of me.

I was feeling peaceful about it, but I was entering a new phase—back in the unknown and a bit off balance as change was under way. I was also feeling the lightness—the presence of the light—that has been lit in my soul always, even when it seemed to be the tiniest flicker and at risk of being extinguished. A couple of years earlier when I was on a sojourn with my friends Yvonne St. John-Dutra and Rich Dutra-St. John, founders of Challenge Day and authors of *Be the Hero You've Been Waiting For*, deep in the land of the ancient Mayan ruins of Mexico and Belize, we had found our way into the belly of Mother Earth and into a darkened cave. It was as black as black can be. We lit a candle to begin our ritual and then blew it out to dwell for a time in this womb of darkness. As I sang a Sanskrit chant I had learned from my time at Sai Baba's ashram in celebration of the mother's love, I swear I could still see a glimmer of the light from the blown-out candle. Maybe it was an optical illusion or the halo effect of the eyes. Or maybe it was confirmation that darkness is merely the absence of light, just as fear is the absence of love, and that my own inner light was still present and would be as long as I was in human form. What it felt like deep down was that I was glimpsing grace—and, in the absence of fear, that I was being guided forward, toward the hope, the endless possibilities, and the healing that the light holds with great love.

At this stage of your healing journey, you, too, may feel off balance as something in you emerges. You may be crouched in your cave of healing, a cocoon of nesting, waiting for any clue that you can progress forward. More and more, you're emerging into the light, and your gifts are birthing. When you step out into the light after being in the darkness, you have to squint a little bit. It takes time for your eyes to adjust, and then everything looks bright and beautiful. Awakening feels like that. Even in the midst of your sorrow, you awaken and everything is breathtaking. It's as if everything is followed by an exclamation mark. Everything is elevated, reminiscent of an Ecstasy trip of my youth or other peak experiences I've had.

In the cave that day in Mexico, my eyes opened and adjusted to more light. They had to. I had to see so I could find the desire and courage to want to live and embark on a new adventure. I continued to have the courage to ask, *What now? Show me the way.*

THE HOOP OF FIRE

Courage doesn't make the uncertainty and vulnerable feelings we have disappear, but it can give us the ignition switch that it takes to move ahead, to not be glued to the floor of our despair. The universe rewards us for taking the steps that are difficult. As hard as they are, and as much as I don't want to take them sometimes, I'm rewarded when I do. I want to emphasize the potential rewards, because at this point, you have made amazing progress, but in some ways, you might also feel stuck. Yet your heart whispers to you that it's not enough merely to survive your loss; you must push forward to thrive.

You know you need to move forward. You might not realize, though, that what you actually have to do is emerge from the emotional and spiritual place where you are being kept alive, just surviving, a place that feels comfortable and safe but where you are so unmoving you begin to feel anxious. You know that becoming stagnant won't really shield you from life. But here you are. Being stuck equates to living your life in the "waiting room," Christina Rasmussen's poignant term for that place of limbo where you can exist in a kind of homeostasis, "not here, not there." You may feel caught between two worlds right now, waiting for something to happen. But it's not like the DMV, where your number will eventually be called (even if it feels like an eternity!) and you will get the license renewal you came for; nobody can push you out of your safe zone. Your therapist, friend, mentor, or partner can encourage you to a door to leave this place of waiting, but only you can take the steps necessary to walk ahead. The victim doesn't take the chance and push forward, but the hero knows that it is necessary to do so.

You must take it upon yourself to move in small steps, leaving your safe place, knowing you can return anytime. Remember that growth is not linear or one step forward after the other. It is stepping in *all* directions that represents freedom. You are fully free to choose. And as you emerge from your cocoon, you will naturally move into and through your fears. But remember, you can do this. No fear is bigger than your heroic heart.

Courage is not the absence of fear; it is stepping forward anyway. Fear is something we all have to deal with in order to progress. The first two steps to breaking free of its hold are to distinguish what kind of fear it is (real or imagined) and then find the limiting beliefs that gave birth to it.

There is physical fear and intuition, both of which act as our guidance systems (turn left, take the next flight, don't sign that contract, leave the relationship, run!, etc.), and then there is emotional fear. Of course, our body, heart, and inner knowing are all intimately intertwined, but often our emotional fears are more connected to the past than the present. That doesn't, however, make them any less valid. They arise from a part of us that is still wounded and is seeking resolution and healing.

Regardless of where a fear is sourced, some fears are useful, even lifesaving, while others are of the toxic emotional kind. Identifying our fears and disentangling from them can feel overwhelmingly complex. It's no wonder we want to hang out in our comfy cave a while longer. I have come to unravel life one question at a time, often starting with these questions: *Where is this fear coming from? Where do I feel it in my body? What is it here to show me?*

When intuition is guiding me to be physically safe, I listen to that. Or intuition often guides me as I read the motives of people I meet. But sometimes I feel fear that causes me some kind of emotional setback or bitch-blocks me from moving forward, and I've learned to become leery of following those kinds of instructions as "inner guidance." That's when I know unhealthy ego is present. My friend Alana Leigh, who has been fervently studying *A Course in Miracles*, says, "Ego is in the house!"

I've come to understand that my emotional fear is actually my best internal guide to reveal to me my most important actions and steps that will lead to my soul's greatest expression, and ultimately my greatest joy and fulfillment. The worst anxiety is knowing that it's time to move forward but feeling like I am, once again, standing on the precipice of the Grand Canyon—again asking the question *What now?* Knowing that the voice of my unhealthy ego causes resistance and confusion in me by manufacturing fear of the unknown makes it super-easy to identify when ego is present and "in the house," doing its best to issue instructions to sabotage any movement forward and keeping me feeling stuck. Stuck in the routine of safety. Stuck waiting for life to happen.

I've learned not to give my power away to that voice of ego, but rather to lean in with greater intensity and access the courage I need to uncover what's behind the fear that's holding me back. To listen deeply to the whisper and the gift present behind the fear. When I don't listen, fear becomes a door with an imaginary hoop of fire (that's ego) around it. Ego makes daily life a matter of high drama, and extra scary. Ego (to me) is the opposite of courage. It is the voice of a coward. The ego mind would like me to stay in the status quo, and not question the way things are. Ego would like to confine me to a box for safekeeping—an empty and colorless room with no windows. Ego would have me wait for a very long time for life to happen. But I am far more courageous than that—and so, my friend, are you! This understanding is a game-changer—a whole new way to emerge and navigate your way forward. Ego shows you where you most need to lean into your fear, jump through the hoop of fire, and step out the door into your journey to wholeness.

Having faced my own formidable and unsettling fears, I have a simple process for stepping through the hoop of fire and opening the door into love and my true essence. It's a process of inquiry for accessing the courage to call out the ego-coward and call on the voice of my true nature. Yes, it's that powerful! And it has been an integral part of my finding my personal holy grail. I've used this process to help others find the gift of their message as well, which is one of the most rewarding aspects of the mentoring I do. Let me tell you why.

Your holy grail is truly the wind beneath your wings. It is your spiritual calling, your sacred purpose in this life. Even before you consciously know what it is, you sense its presence. It's your own reason why you are here, and often it comes through your most difficult passages—in times of suffering. As you have grown, it has grown, too. You feel its gravitational pull. And you sense that it has carried you through those times when you could barely move. Far more than a metaphor, your holy grail is your *aliveness*, bubbling up from the wellspring of your soul. Aliveness, passion, and purpose are inextricable from one another and tied to the divine spirit and source of life from which we all come. My hope is that by the time you close this book you will never feel separated from them again.

As you feel and as you heal, you are guided by such love and grace, and you will be rewarded for your inner work in facing your fears and walking through the fire. You will emerge tenderly, albeit feeling like a newborn fawn on wobbly feet.

I think that one of the most moving aspects of the quest for the holy grail—your quest—is that it promises you will find what has never been found before, because what you will find can only arise in and come through *you*. Every time you feel the desire to step into something bigger—a vocation, a relationship, a way of being that demands your deepest truth, wisdom, and love—you are having a holy-grail moment.

Bringing the light of your awareness to your fears is an important step in beginning to find (or further clarify) your purpose—in claiming your holy grail. Awareness is the only requirement at this point. You'll have an opportunity to write about your fear in the Soul Inquiry section below. For now, all you need to do is take my hand and turn toward the fears that are keeping you stuck.

THE HOOP OF FIRE PROCESS

- *Stop and breathe. Sit quietly, sensing the place of stillness within you.*
- *Put one hand on your belly and the other on your heart, and let your body know that you are willing to listen to its wisdom. Then ask your body what it has to say to you.*
- *Tune in to your physical sensations. How does it feel to breathe in deeply? Is your solar plexus tight? Are your shoulders or neck sore? Where are you tense? Where are you holding something?*
- *Now let yourself touch the feelings beneath the bodily sensations that may be masking your fear. Ask yourself:* What am I feeling? Is it confusion? Doubt? Anxiety? Dread?
- *How do these feelings keep you in the "waiting room"? Ask yourself:* What is the fear (ego) trying to tell me not to do? *How is fear creating a block between you and a dream you have for your life?*
- *Now name the hoop of fire. Is it self-doubt? Is it "I'm not worthy of joy"? Is it fear of rejection or fear of failure? Or is it fear of your success? What is the painfully limiting belief that spits fire at you at the threshold of your future?*

Sandra is a woman in her midforties who felt her biological clock ticking—not for birthing children but for birthing her true love. After this latest breakup, a relationship of two years, she was freaked out by the possibility of being alone and not finding "the love of her life." Her heartbreak came from grieving a future she expected was out there and thought she wasn't finding. She started dating and looking for serious love far too soon to be ready—to be whole. Every time it didn't work out with some guy, she rushed back into dating, not taking the time to be on the journey to heal into wholeness. Sandra needed to face the fear of being alone with courage, intention, and integrity. A person who is afraid of being alone will have to jump through the hoop of fire and lean into the fear of being alone by choosing to spend some quality time on their own. It took a few months, but by jumping through the hoop, spending this time with the intention of not dating someone for distraction, Sandra realized that the most important relationship is the one she has with herself, and learning to love her own company was the first step to leaning in.

I know a man, Larry, in his fifties, who was so happy when he opened his small hardwood-flooring company. He hummed along for years and enjoyed all the aspects of running his own company, but then the 2008 world financial crisis happened. Building came to a halt, and he lost everything. Despondent for a time, he felt like he might be perceived as too old to enter the job market, and for a long time he had little desire to do so. He was afraid that he would be outdated and unable to find a job, and his fears paralyzed him. Then one day the phone rang. A friend called Larry and invited him to take his dog to the dog park. At the park, Larry had a conversation with another man. Larry asked why the man wasn't working, and he exclaimed, "Oh, I'm working. I'm just working my own hours and my own schedule. I'm an independent contractor for an insurance company." Larry's wheels started spinning, and his interest was piqued. His enthusiasm rose even higher when his new friend told him how gratifying it was to make sure families were protected with life insurance when they lost a loved one. In that industry, it could be to your benefit to be in midlife because you have the wisdom that comes with age to add to your credibility as an adviser. Larry leaned into the fear that he was too old and stepped through his hoop of fire to discover a new career that was gratifying to him in new ways.

When you lean into your greatest emotional fear—not intuition or physical fear related to a clear and present danger—when you move toward it, right behind it is a great gift. It's the expression of your soul. It's the reason you came to this world. It's where you are who you are, unequivocally and without apology. It's where you get to have a party with yourself. *Wheeeeee! Oh, this is what it feels like to be* me*! How cool! I've been waiting a long time for this. This* is *who I am! (Did I really have to go through all of* that *to get here?!)* Your unhealthy ego doesn't do well with that. It shrieks at you (in a very high, squeaky voice), "*Noooooooooooooooooo!* You could be destroyed! You will make a fool of yourself! And people will laugh at you!" The ego assures that you'll get a banana cream pie in your face and that all of that whipped cream might hurt! In other words, the ego is absolutely absurd, and you will recognize the insanity of its screams. But this is not the time in your journey for giving in to your fears; you're emerging through them now. This is the point in the epic movie of your life where audience members are shouting at the big screen, trying to get your attention, awaken you from the nightmare, and cheer you on: "Don't believe that little voice! It's lying to you! You're almost there! Don't you dare give up now!"

You are stepping into what feels like the great unknown. And you are going to land in freedom.

SOMETIMES WE CRAWL

I was visiting my retreat home at Sea Ranch, and as I was taking a walk, I felt distracted by the news I had heard earlier that day of a young woman who had committed suicide. I knew of her, as she had graduated from my daughter's high school and college. Feeling sad for this family dealing with this news, I was stepping up a rocky trail and, uncharacteristically, given my usual surefootedness, I lost my balance. As I instinctively tried to course-correct, my foot came down hard and broke, propelling me backward off the rock. Fortunately, my good friend Shauna was right behind me. As if in slow motion, she was able to brace herself while grabbing my arm and breaking my fall. I had gone away for a weekend of writing and meditation and found myself in an urgent-care facility.

Now, my broken right foot confirmed with an X-ray, I ponder what this means as I begin to write a chapter—where I propose that you are ready to stand on your two feet, emerging, while I am able to use only one. My, oh my, doesn't the universe have a sense of humor? Louise Hay, author of *Heal Your Body,* the beloved healing reference guide, says a broken toe or foot means not wishing to move forward. In my case, my broken foot has shown up to slow me down, as I've been moving forward way too fast.

What I've noticed in this more fragile way of life, often crawling on the floor to get where I needed to go in the early days of healing, is that slowing down becomes an opportunity to sink into my experience of being present and mindful in new ways, deepening my compassion for what it feels like to live disabled. I am also reminded of how disabled I felt at times when I was grieving. Now, physically injured, I was sitting in my favorite chair listening to the birds wake up the other morning. I had scooted my coffee cup over from the kitchen on a bar stool with great labor while using my crutches. (You don't have use of your hands while on crutches! And this was a few days before I rented my sexy scooter.) As I sat there, I asked, *Why has this shown up for me?* The answer was so clear.

As my love of life is my most devoted partner these days, not too unlike when we are in a marriage where one feels taken for granted, this misstep and fall on the trail causing my broken foot has served as a reminder of how everything is here to deepen my interaction with my experience. I'm learning a new kind of mindfulness in my body through nursing and protecting my foot. In this way, my intimacy with my life experience is deepening as I open up to the healing presenting me with this new learning. Just as we see into our partner, we have the same opportunity to partner with life—and to see into all that comes to us, the joy and all the other stuff. "Seeing into" what comes means meeting our life events and circumstances with a willingness to understand, grow, and sometimes to change. It means meeting our life with tenderness, vulnerability, and trust, seeing into life with an open heart.

What if the hardships and heartbreaks you face are *all* happening for your emergence? You choose to be the hero at every event by seeing the story of your life unfold in and as the mystery. Remember that this breakup, this broken limb, this broken career, this broken dream, this broken anything is here to assist you in breaking the barriers to love—a love that will wake you, it's so inspiring. A love that will show all things, and your interactions with the circumstances presented to you, as divine. A love that will carry you through as you continue to emerge, leaving you feeling happy for no reason.

WE DON'T MOVE ON; WE CARRY THEM FORWARD

Sitting under the heat lamps with my hair twisted in foil, fortunately unrecognizable and very alien looking, waiting for my highlights to happen, I began a conversation with a woman who was having her hair cut by a young man who happened to be my previous hairdresser (the one I escaped to on my grief-stricken days years ago). I can only imagine that Dan was listening and remembering how I was in those days when I came in grieving and quiet. He was perfect for me and just allowed me my silence. He was slow, too. Interestingly, getting my hair done was one of the only outings I allowed myself in those early days.

The woman and I were talking about a concert that was happening at the Greek Theatre in Berkeley on Friday—Earth, Wind & Fire was coming. She said, "My friends really want me to go, but I'm not feeling up to it. I lost my grandmother, my best friend, a few months ago, and everyone feels like I should move on already. I just feel like I don't know how to live without her." I told her that I understood, and it turned out she had heard me speak at a women's event a few years earlier for my book *Don't Sweat the Small Stuff for Moms*.

"You know, you don't have to move on from your grandmother, and what if she isn't actually gone?" I said.

She raised her eyebrows—as I noticed Dan lowering his head a little—and burst into tears.

She said, "Please go on and explain what you mean." I replied, "When a person dies, they leave their body, but what if they can be anywhere without a body? Where do you think your grandmother would be if she could be anywhere?" The woman responded softly, "My grandmother would be right here with me." I said, "She most certainly would—especially if you invite her. Your relationship with her doesn't have to die with her body. You must find a new way to relate to her in her new form. You can carry her with you now."

In great loss, one of the realizations I had that changed the game of healing for me was that I did not have to "move on" and live without Richard. My relationship with him could continue on, and I would carry him with me. That realization helped me to emerge into a new life. As I would think of him, I could feel he was right beside me—steadfast as always, my loyal companion now formless. We don't move on, we move forward, mindfully aware of our loved one's presence with us. Resiliency comes from knowing, in the deep well of our soul, that the love we share is eternal and transcends the boundaries of time and space.

In the same way, we can continue loving someone even through a breakup. During a recent breakup with a lover and dear friend, in our no-contact phase, which took us years to have the courage to face, I have been closing my eyes and sending him love. I see myself in a white-light circle, and he is in one, too, just touching mine but not overlapping. I welcome him and tell him everything I wish him to know. I visualize a neon-blue figure eight moving clockwise around him and counterclockwise around me to separate our psychic energy in a healthy way. Then I push his bubble away, sending him off and into divine consciousness. I open my eyes and feel peace and love for him—grateful for the time we spent together.

It has taken time to arrive at this opening. Back in 2016, at the ten-year anniversary of Richard's death, I was reaching some completion, but I wasn't quite there yet. My own "waiting room" is around embracing true partnership again—even after ten years. When you're a widow, and you had a wonderful relationship and marriage with your husband, it leaves you feeling like your cup is still half full. The other half has more to do with my physical needs than anything else, and some emotional support and companionship. It's easy to settle for half of what you need when your cup is still half full from what you had.

While I was feeling a new sense of wholeness, emotionally there was still some letting go to do—and some deep fear of letting go remained. Author Spencer Johnson says, "Change happens when the pain of holding on becomes greater than the fear of letting go." That quote truly resonates in my heart and soul. When I think about the crutches, Band-Aids, and emotional tourniquets I've used to survive and to be able to continue my life, I can see now that even something that has served a function becomes dysfunctional and codependent when there is no truth being told. I had a very special relationship and love connection that served me so well and so beautifully for many years, as I believe it served him, too. But after years of being tied at the feet, attempting to move forward without the true commitment of partnership, our connection needed to shift. It's easy to fall into the habit of being with someone who feels so comfortable. Yet our relationship was becoming a drain on both of us, tying our energy up in ways that wasn't healthy for either of us.

Letting go of this companion, after nine years of far more than a dating relationship, for me, is another milestone step along the hero's journey. No longer sitting and waiting for something that doesn't fit to change, I'm reminded of the wise words of Buddhist teacher Jack Kornfield. "In the end, these things matter most: How well did you love? How fully did you live? How gratefully did you live? How deeply did you let go?" We were and are healers and a loving balm for one another—a safe place to land. Many relationships can be wonderful, healing connections, but I made the all-too-common mistake of falling in love with the potential of what could be versus feeling into what it actually was. As a positive person, it's easy for me to envision the most positive scenario and allow a person the space to grow into that. I would say to myself, "Be patient, Kris. When he opts in, he'll know how powerful this can be." But finally, it became clear that a committed relationship was not what was in our design— at least not at this time, and I could not wait any longer. As I began dating other men, I was acutely aware that my heart was holding back and my love still had a placeholder attached, even though I could feel he had moved on. I began to realize that in my dangling wait I could be bypassing something new that was also waiting for me. And I was right. Over the years, I had let a lot of men pass by me—really good men. I held steady in my "waiting room," in the relationship that was "not here, not there." The paradox is that the "waiting room" both held me and held me back from moving forward.

As I began to write this book for you, I knew I had to take this final step and let go of this loving man I adored for so many reasons. It was perfect for what I needed all those years, and I'm so grateful for that time with him. I believed that letting go for a time would help me make that leap into a new connection with him, one that would let us meet in a healthier place as true friends. The time had come for me to step away—to pull off all the bandages, to drop the crutches, and see that I can walk on my own (or crawl for a while, as the case may be, as my one foot dangles now). I'm OK. I'm whole. I'm complete. I don't need to hold on out of fear. I can be in this space of standing on my own two feet. The wound of my loss of Richard is a scar now, a crack healed by gold, making me wiser and more truth-telling. My heart is mended now, and my heartache a soft reminder of another life. There are always tears for parts of the journey, there is longing for my love, but my heart is definitely buoyant now as I've discovered a whole new way to love. Every day I'm ready to take on life as a new adventure. To be in joy no matter what I am doing. To seize the day and to love my life and my own company.

GOING AFTER YOUR HOLY GRAIL

A sign that you are ready to emerge is when you find yourself asking, *What now?* You are done with the initiations and ready to shore everything up in your life. You are fully embracing all of it and ready to lean into your new life with the spirit of adventure—and in hot pursuit of your holy grail. To do this, you must realize who you are, and who you are no longer, and know deep within that you are enough, just as you are. The hero's journey that you have embarked upon *is* this journey of self-realization. The power of the human spirit to persevere is the energy you will tap into in order to make the leap—out of suffering and into greater joy. Nelson Mandela said, "The power of the human spirit is not that we don't fall down, the power of the human spirit is we get back up—every time we fall."

Be assured that the countless number of times you've gotten back up to your feet, and the steps you have already taken, and will continue to take, will lead you to the edge where you will leap—where your new dream begins. Transformation rarely seems to happen with a big running start, like in the movies. Change is often quieter than that. And I would venture to say that the qualities required to take big leaps are the very same qualities needed to get back up and take the small steps: courage, commitment, intention, integrity, acceptance, and self-love. These are the qualities of the spiritual warrior that you have become—and the hero you are choosing to be.

At this stage of your journey, you have looked for and found the "message in the mess"—the gift that comes to you as a revelation from deep within the heart of your loss. Mine was the gift of *feeling* my life. This time of emergence is when you move out and beyond identifying the gift of what has happened to you and begin to articulate its meaning. It's when you're able to see more clearly than ever what this heartbreak has opened up in you. As your clarity sharpens, and as you connect the dots that make sense of what has at times seemed senseless, your purpose comes into clearer focus, too (a topic that we will fully delve into in the next chapter). You don't need to work too hard to figure all of this out, either; just let it show itself to you. A branding expert once told me that I could now create myself as whoever I wanted to be. "No," I responded. "I won't create myself, but I will reveal myself."

Just as you are emerging, so is the meaning and purpose of your story. And as you own that story, you won't be able to help but share it with other people. The desire to give, serve, and contribute will increase—becoming more like a need. We learn through story, and stories are passed along to teach and inspire small children, teenagers, and adults alike. Whether you share your story with one person or millions of people, sharing it helps the whole of humanity; it helps connect us to one heart. We are all drops in the same ocean. One person may be all you need to reach. In an interview not long before her death, Mother Teresa said, "Jesus did not say, 'Love the whole world.' He said, 'Love one another.' You can only love one person at a time. If you look at the numbers, you get lost. While you are talking about hunger, somebody is dying next to you."

As I shared in the opening pages of this book, I had to go through my initiations and heart lessons so that I would say yes to my purpose and open my arms fully to why I came to this earth. Before life cracked me open in the ways that it has, I was as perplexed as anyone about what my true purpose is. But I am very clear now. And I know that this kind of yes is a life-changing yes. Through the peaks and valleys, what drives me forward is knowing that I am a vehicle of divine light and love. What I realized is that I couldn't wake up and then fully go back to sleep again, and you won't, either. Your purpose—that beautiful fire in your soul—will continually send you signs and smoke signals. It will knock on the door of your reality over and over. If you frequently find yourself awake and staring at the ceiling in the wee hours of the morning, it's probably the call of your soul. You can call it insomnia or a case of too much coffee or having a lot on your mind, but it's probably your deepest purpose asking you to live it.

My client Deanna is feeling this call. Forty-three years old and accomplished, Deanna is an extremely creative person—in tune to divine guidance and one of those people who has ideas like "popcorn" (that's how she describes it): a steady flow of creative bursts that come after a process of meditation and surrender. She taps into this stream, surrenders her mind, and is open to receiving creative ideas and insights. For years, as a single mom, she was always concerned with putting food on the table. She applied her creativity to her work, but it wasn't quite the right vehicle for her spirit for a variety of reasons, so she had to let it go. Closing her business, marrying her new love, and a year of soul-searching on her own led her to a daylong intensive mentoring session with me where we set about clarifying and articulating her purpose in relationship to her work in the world. "I am emerging now," Deanna said to me as we looked together at the mind map I had written on the flip chart in front of us. The way I see it, the themes and action plans sketched out on the page form a treasure map pointing toward Deanna's holy grail, toward her embarking on a new path and allowing what is within to be revealed and discovered—to be seen and heard.

We are born perfectly capable of doing one thing, and that one thing is to be ourselves. The beauty of what is discovered as you peel back the layers of fear is that there's nothing to do to be who you are. Through our lives and those limiting beliefs that form, we stop emerging as we are born to be, and we morph and change into some wax version of ourselves. Sometimes, our passion, joy, and purpose get buried under layers of hurt and confusion. But that is a game of hide-and-seek we don't want to play for too long; it's just too painful. A heart can break time and time again, and yet—if we are willing to lean into our fears and let go of the pain, leaping fully through the hoop of fire—our heart heals, and new life awaits.

Remember, this time period has been about healing your heart, but now you are deeply feeling the need to step forward in your life—

and stop waiting for life to happen. You are called to action to lean into your fears and to begin to mindfully move forward in baby steps, while realizing the gifts that have brought you to the doorway of change. You are ready to embrace the lessons learned and the new adventure ahead. You are emerging now, and there is something emerging from within you that is ready to be seen. You are feeling more you than you ever have before—let's discover and reveal more.

> ## SOUL MANTRA:
>
> Meditate on this soul affirmation and mantra for five minutes:
>
> *I will lean into my fear that has shown up to guide me. I can move forward now.*

....

THE SOUL INQUIRY:
THROUGH THE HOOP OF FIRE

Pull out your journal and answer these questions vulnerably.

1. What are my deepest emotional fears?
2. Where is fear present in my body?
3. Where am I stuck in my life?
4. What feelings are holding me back?
5. What is my hoop of fire—the number one thing I feel most afraid to do, but that I know I need to do?
6. What do I need in order to feel safe to move forward?

....

Your New Story • *transformational writing process*

What now? Write about what would most like to come forward now. What wants to be revealed? What wants to emerge? What is your holy grail, your spiritual calling? What is it that has the power to move you from emotional pain, procrastination, or inertia into action, giving you the energy to leap through your hoop of fire?

_____

_____

_____

_____

_____

_____

_____

_____

_____

_____

_____

_____

_____

_____

_____

_____

_____

_____

_____

_____

The Alchemy of Change

The Promise of Chapter 7—You will see your story as the gold that has come through the alchemical process of healing your heart. Here is where you will define your life purpose—giving your journey greater meaning.

In the weeks after Richard's death, our web master started to accept tributes from various friends and other authors to post on our *dontsweat.com* website. Our site was suddenly receiving hundreds of thousands of hits a day as condolences poured in from all over the world. I read them every day, finding comfort from the ways that Richard had impacted others. But then one post came up that completely knocked me off my feet. It was written by a woman who was a friend of Richard's in his graduate course work. He had gone overnight from starving author to being invited everywhere, and it was overwhelming to say the least. Speaking requests and media bookings were coming in at ten to twenty requests per day, and he needed some temporary help. She was in limbo in her own career, and Richard invited her to help him for a short time. My intuition always warned me that she had deeper feelings than friendship for him. In my mind, I thought, *Who wouldn't have them?* He was so kind and loving and present. I am not a jealous woman, but my husband was a bit naïve with women, so I brought it up several times to him, asking him to remain guarded. Years later, he did finally concede that it was possible that she had feelings for him that exceeded what was acceptable to the boundaries of their friendship; she relocated, and he put some emotional distance between them.

It was during this vulnerable time for my family, shortly after the memorial celebration, that she wrote an extremely inappropriate tribute that insinuated a far deeper connection of friendship. While it's true I was feeling sensitive, possibly overly sensitive, even though it's likely that it was unintentional, her words cut through me, as sharp as a knife could feel. I was devastated and furious that she could be so insensitive to me and the girls at this fragile time.

I sat in front of my computer screen, stunned. I have never known such irreconcilable feelings in my mind, heart, and body as this incident produced. Words can hurt as much as any physical slap. I've never known such complete and utter devastation. After reading this "tribute" that somehow put the sanctity of my marriage and relationship in question, I lay in my bed broken and yearning for Richard's reassurance that this was only a one-sided misstep by this woman, with one-sided feelings. It was this incident, however, that tore down a veil between dimensions, allowing grace to hold me in a way that has forever changed me.

My vision at first was blurred by a torrent of tears, and I squeezed my eyes tight as I sobbed. Just as I was feeling more alone than I could ever remember, I began to feel a warmth surround me, like being held in the folds of a heated blanket. As I was drawn into this swaddled hug, suddenly a calm peace came over me. I opened my eyes; the room melted into orange atoms, and all objects appeared in beautiful golden waves. I was suspended in this embrace as all forms in the room melted into a glow of orange. Then the most brilliant light came to me. It was so bright, it appeared to be sunlight with liquid mercury in the center creating a bright silver luminescence—the most magnificent light I've ever seen. For many seconds, I sat in awe of this sacred presence and the tender words of assurance that Richard had for me in telepathy.

"Oh, my love, know that this was only her grief and her fear. I love you with all of my heart, and there is no truth but that. I am here with you where I'll always be."

I had received divine assistance at a time I most needed it. Grace had come to me in one of my most pain-wrought moments, early on, bringing my beloved close. My love knew that I had to be jettisoned out of that fear, that moment, as fast as possible. It was a defining moment. I could have gotten stuck in that place of doubt and despair, and it would have changed everything. It would have altered my story—the one I would tell myself. But grace came to reassure me of the purity of Richard's heart so I could be free of this torment and know that our love was true—so that I could be comforted and open to heal and to carry on, and to live. There was nothing to question. Everything came to me in that moment to help me move into this heroine's journey *so* quickly and immediately.

I began a new relationship with Richard, and I could feel his energy, like a heart contracting, come close to me, where I could feel the bliss of being one with him before he expanded further into his journey—leaving me with a feeling of emptiness that at first was terrifying but allowed me to grieve. Beat by beat, grace was saying: "You are meant to know that the love of your life was and is the love of your life. No woman can bring that into question. Not now, not ever."

Grace often comes unbidden to regenerate and restore us when we're disoriented by crisis and loss. Kate, the woman I wrote about earlier who had been violently attacked, shared one of her precious moments of grace with me. Three days after fighting for her life in her darkened bedroom, now safe from harm, she had grown restless from being indoors and walked to a coffeehouse a few blocks from the place of refuge she had found with a dear friend—of course, she could not stay in the apartment that had become a place of terror. Still numb and in shock, she took her latte and muffin to a table in the middle of the café, wanting to be surrounded by the comforting hum of people talking about normal things helping to ease the trauma of her anything but normal life.

Just minutes after she took her seat, a man in a wheelchair rolled up to Kate's table and asked if he could join her, given the limited seating on this busy morning. She recognized him right away. It was Ron Kovic, the former U.S. Marine sergeant paralyzed in the Vietnam War whose memoir *Born on the Fourth of July* became an Academy Award–winning film starring Tom Cruise. She told him that she recognized him and that she had been deeply affected and inspired by his story. Although shaking on the inside as she felt the soul-level importance of this "chance" encounter, she attempted to make small talk for the first few minutes, keeping her sunglasses on to hide the whites of her eyes, which were completely red from having hemorrhaged in the battle with her intruder. But the layer of skin that had been scraped from her chin and cheek left a visible wound that invited a mild investigation from a wounded warrior such as this.

"Would you be willing to take off your sunglasses?" Ron asked her in a kind voice.

"*What* happened to you?" he asked as Kate's glasses reached the tabletop.

In these fragile first days following the incident, Kate was in awe of the rare opportunity to ask this true hero what he had done to lift himself from the hole of devastation after the shock of a lifetime.

"How did you deal with it? When your life was abruptly, violently changed in one moment, what did you do to not let it take you all the way down?" she questioned him.

She wanted to know how it was that he had chosen to be the hero rather than a victim, sensing that her future depended on listening closely to what he had to say. Grace brought this perfect messenger to her, at a moment when Kate's entire being was reverberating with horror and shock, and nothing less than deep soul guidance would do, from someone who would understand her heartbreak. Kate had always believed that her life had meaning and now urgently needed to find meaning in her crisis. Grace brought this meeting so that Kate could immediately opt into her heroine's journey.

I understand that. I believe in the love that Richard and I share so deeply, and still I was vulnerable and deeply shaken. I felt defenseless. He was defenseless. But when I opened my eyes to a film of golden, vibrating mercurial wonder, feeling incredibly loved, I was just in it. This alive radiance was so breathtaking, so warm. It filled my whole body with love, and I felt immediate relief. Grace had once again shown me the power of surrendering—the true solace of opening to being held and divinely guided. And I felt so grateful that I had that reassurance and could rest in the truth, where love transcends everything.

LIVING ALCHEMY—TRANSMUTING BROKENNESS INTO BEAUTY

Something changed for me that devastating day of that tribute. A transformation happened: My anguish and pain were transmuted into peace. This was my first true experience of personal alchemy. In the Middle Ages, alchemy was both a science and a philosophy devoted to finding an elixir for life—a panacea for curing all ills. In this quest, alchemists explored methods for transmuting base metals into gold. In other words, they could change one substance into something entirely new. Centuries later, the great psychologist Carl Jung found parallels between the science of alchemy and the sacred process of becoming a whole human being. He recognized the inner alchemy where the mix of one's imagination, dreams, and visions—the unconscious archetypal forces—is medicine for the mending of the soul. With the merging of our many wounds and losses, spirit and matter are divinely knitted together.

In the Japanese art of fixing broken pottery known as "kintsugi," dating back to the fifteenth century, a vessel or other object that has been cracked or broken into pieces is repaired with a special lacquer mixed with powdered gold, silver, or platinum. As a philosophy, kintsugi embraces the flaws and imperfections of a cup, bowl, vase, or other piece, seeing the cracks and subsequent repairs as inevitable events in the life of an object and not flaws that render it less valuable or useless. It views both the breakage and the repair as parts of the rich and unique story of an object rather than something to conceal. Perhaps most poignantly, kintsugi celebrates as beautiful what we have been conditioned to view as defects—blemishes, structural weaknesses, or the disfigurements of age. Each fracture and chip is lovingly suffused with the artist's care with every brushstroke of resin made of gold or another precious metal.

In this one devastating tribute, I had been shown something powerful. I had begun to experience the real alchemy of change that would open my perception to new dimensions and help me to step into the fullness of my mission while continuing my relationship with my beloved. I had been held and bathed in the shimmering mercury-silver light of love, as it filled in the cracks of my broken heart and opened my mind—allowing more light into what was going to be my dark night of the soul. I was going down fast, but help arrived when I needed it, and I am forever grateful.

Every bit of my heartbreak is a part of my history—the chronicling of my soul's path. And the more I live and the more I love, I see gratitude as the real change agent. Gratitude is an expression of joy that creates the lasting changes in us. It's the gold that holds and strengthens us and tumbles our soul as we ascend from the unimaginable moments of loss and loneliness into feelings of peace and fullness. Our light becomes more brilliant as we heal, and we become even more beautiful in our humanity and our compassion. It's realizing our blessings amidst adversity that carries us—this is what carried me. My history was one of building a great life with a great man, and I held on to the blessing of our lives together as I stepped into the journey.

This same alchemy of change can happen in a long-term marriage or partnership. Over the years, your connection may have had some weak links and you may have drifted. I know of two couples who had similar scenarios, where one of the partners was unfaithful. While there were many emotions that needed to be reconciled and resolved in their marriages, they were able to stand stronger as they repaired the cracks of their commitment and to remain together as they chose to claim their lives with a fresh start. Richard always said, "If people only knew what a ninety-day sabbatical would mean to their work, their marriage . . ." In the time you take to reflect on what's right, often what's wrong falls away. Sometimes, all we need is the boost of a fresh start to realize all that we already have to be grateful for. While many couples don't make it through infidelity, both of these couples remain married and have rekindled the spark that had gone dormant. Through forgiveness, and referring to the blessings of their lives and their history, they have decided to expand into a greater love—one that will carry them forward.

In this same way, you can now see that your heartbreak is part of your history, too. You no longer need to feel weakened by your loss because the clarity, wisdom, and depth of your hero's journey have revealed gifts and blessings to you amidst change. To take what has been broken in you and repair it with your own alchemical blend makes it all—your whole life—even more vibrant and stunning. One might say that your true beauty is revealed in your chipped and repaired state. Perhaps you are becoming more yourself than ever before from this broken place, where the cracks allow more light to come in . . . and to stream back out into the world through your broken-open heart. You may even feel larger from the alchemy of the gratitude you feel for having endured this time of change, inviting grace to hold you.

HOW TO CHANGE YOUR LIFE

Richard's father, Don W. Carlson, exemplified how to live a life of gratitude. Don was a great man who lived well and loved big. He was profoundly humble about his humanness, yet he showed up as big as his 6'5" frame. In his college days, he was a three-time letterman at Stanford University and at Cal Berkeley. He played basketball in the U.S. Army, where he also held the service's physical fitness record. In the eighties, he went on to become a real estate mogul who believed in personal growth for his hundreds of employees, bringing progressive speakers like Ram Dass and Stephen Levine to his company. He helped build an organization called BENS (Business Executives for National Security), involving Ted Turner and Shirley MacLaine, that was instrumental in ending the Cold War with Russia. He visited Russia as a diplomatic gesture and coauthored a book with Craig Comstock called *Citizen Summitry: Keeping the Peace When It Matters Too Much to Be Left to Politicians*. He also ran and funded the Ark philanthropic foundation for many years. After he sold his real-estate company, his fortune was greatly diminished by legal battles. As a major shareholder, Don held on to his own shares as an act of solidarity with the people he had enrolled into his general partnerships while many of the top shareholders cashed out to preserve their own interests. In other words, Don Carlson was a man of heart who was also as generous as any person could be. He didn't care much about the stuff money could buy; he made his fortune only to give most of it away.

For all of his accomplishments, however (and there are too many to list here), I have never been so impressed with anyone as I was with him in the last two years of his life. His gratitude and his love of life continued even though he had been dealt a hand most of us dread. After a debilitating stroke that left him immobile, except for his head, one hand, and an arm, he lay in bed in complete surrender with a feeding tube, blind from macular degeneration, but his mind intact. What a great mind he had, too, full of the knowledge in thousands of books he had read over the years; he had well-developed opinions on politics and economics and was well informed on all of the great philosophers.

I would visit him often, every day when I could. It felt good to be standing in for Richard. He would have not left his dad's side. Despite all that he had lost, Don once told me, "Kris, I'm so grateful for this life. It's really not that bad lying here. The people caring for me are kind, and my friends come by to see me. And, I'm so grateful for your visits." Even though he was 90 percent blind and required the full-time care of nurses to bathe him and change his diapers, and even though he hadn't had a meal of solid food in a year and a half, his entire being bloomed like a bodhisattva—an ordinary person who understands that the well-being of humanity lives within each one of us and joyously embraces responsibility for the whole. Each time, my heart would break open a little more as I loved his spirit and the gentleness he showed me. His ego had all but dissolved, allowing the purity of his essence to be present.

To me, he had taken on the energy of a true Master of Love. He had lost his son, his wife, and his bodily functions but still was able to talk with people and share his stories. He had shared with me that his life purpose was to have those people with whom he met leave feeling better than when they arrived. In his business days, it would be over coffee, breakfast, or lunch, but now it was as he lay in his bed, open and vulnerable. In fact, his whole life had been an honoring of his life purpose. He even fell in love again before he died, with a woman at the care facility. "The way I see it, I may as well live fully, because I have a long time to be dead," he would tell me.

Don Carlson was in love with life itself and felt the blessing of that—right up until his last breath. When you love life itself—more than any one thing that goes right or wrong—that's when you are living your most resilient and vibrant life.

If you want to change your life, you will find something you're grateful for. If you can attach to your gratitude in every situation, your healing will accelerate. When I first broke my foot, there were a few times when I felt pretty down at the thought of the five to eight weeks the doctor said it would take to heal. Then I would remember how much worse it could have been, and I would feel into the gratitude for all of the help I had during the healing process. After the poor-pitiful-me phase, returning to gratitude made my life so much easier. Again, it was a matter of remembering that surrender into the process is the key, and also focusing my attention on all that I have to be grateful for rather than what I'd be missing as my broken foot mended.

As Don demonstrated, the hero finds joy every day. And when you have a gratitude practice, joy becomes your nature over time. This can be as simple as making a list of ten things in your journal each day that you're grateful for, or not getting out of bed in the morning until you've thought about the three things you're most grateful for in that moment. This can include the simplest graces, such as the sound of songbirds outside your window. What matters most is the feeling that accompanies the thoughts.

DAY-TO-DAY ALCHEMY—THE GOLD OF YOUR LIFE'S PURPOSE

How does the alchemical process happen on the day-to-day level? What are the catalysts for healing change and transformation to take place? Consciously choosing gratitude and joy on a daily basis is a powerful invitation to change and, moreover, a powerful life practice. Life is like a sport. You have to practice it the way you wish to live it and with the feelings you want to have. Joy tends to grow like a weed. It's nurtured by those life-affirming choices that say, *Yes, I'm fully engaged with life! I am* in *the game and willing to allow change to happen and evolve as my life unfolds, no matter what I get. I'm willing to let go when it's in my best interest to do so, and to open myself to the birth of something new.*

Another catalyst for transformation, which we'll go deeper into in the next chapter, is a way of being that I've been practicing for many years. I regularly take myself away from the world and retreat in order to gather myself again. I'm better able to surf the waves of change when I retreat into stillness, feel the rhythm and pulse of my being, and then go back into the world, refreshed and receptive. Although several days away from the busyness and routine of home is ideal, even miniretreats can support a more supple relationship with change. Sitting under a tree in a park for an hour at lunch or walking through your neighborhood in the quiet of dawn or dusk, you can prioritize your inner world in order to meet the outer world with an open heart. Retreating and returning, again and again. Not unlike a heart beating in contractions, you can also relate to life in ebb and flow. As you do this, you are cultivating a deeper connection with the fullness of yourself, right where you are. If you're not already there, you will be learning to love your own company, and you will no longer fear being alone. As the noise of our complex world turns down a few notches, you'll hear the quiet whisper of your heart and feel what's really happening inside, and you will be ready to respond in kind.

One of the most powerful ways to support the alchemy of change at the day-to-day level is captured in the words "this too shall pass" and "carry on"—the perennial wisdom that we discussed in the early stages of preparing for the journey. At nearly every stage in the return to wholeness, this is the perspective of the hero and the heroine. The hero in us knows, deep within, that all things are as temporary as clouds in the sky and all things will pass—*and they will change into something else.* Rather than a somber reality check, it's cause for celebration! The passage of one thing is always the birth of something new.

Knowing and trusting this process gives us the optimism and hope we need to slow down and give life time to unfold magically. We stop avoiding or trying to force change, and we *allow* it instead. However, as our passion is calling us to greater meaning, our purpose suddenly can become clearer. Still, it is important to go through a process and determine an overarching statement that is your life purpose. It's impossible to enter the process fully if we're too distracted and going elsewhere. We have to be the instrument, knowing that this message— this life purpose—is coming through us. Life happens *for* us, not *to* us—all so that who we are and what we're here to do and how we're here to express ourselves can be revealed. Allowing and not rushing to know what might happen next is elegantly summarized in the Taoist idea of "doing, not doing." In order to write this book, for example, I realized that I couldn't fill my schedule with interviews, speaking engagements, and a lot of social activities. I also removed myself from social media (except for a post or two now and then) for several months to be fully present for the creative flow of this book to come through me. If I wanted to "do" this book, I needed to allot time for "not doing," as well.

Of course, breaking my foot in the middle of my writing process gave me more time for "not doing" than I bargained for! I was thrust into figuring out how to redesign my life so that my foot would have the best chance to heal completely and I could avoid surgery. I had my low moments—in chaos for a while, and then bumping up against resistance to the reality of what was happening, and the fact that, unable to drive or walk, I felt trapped and unable to pursue many of my passions. Also, of course, it's always a transition to be forced to slow down. But I knew that the resistance and the angst I was feeling, for about two weeks, meant that I was about to surrender. And I did. I was finally able to sincerely ask myself, *What are the great gifts of this broken foot going to be?* It reminded me of how it feels to be in day one of a long intensive workshop or the beginning of anything long. At first it seems like it's going to drag on, and then suddenly it's five days later, and I've received countless gifts by surrendering to the process and becoming present in it. Once the mind lets go of all the reasons, ideas, and beliefs that keep us stuck, then we get into the flow of letting go. (Remember, save the swimming upstream for the salmon to do—that's worth repeating here!) Of course, slowing down allowed me the much-needed time to write this book that is very much in alignment with my life purpose.

YOUR PURPOSE STATEMENT

It is now time to formulate a statement of your life purpose. The tree below will be used as a metaphor and picture to help you understand that once you develop a statement of your life purpose, you will see that all things you do are considered projects that become branches of your tree. Your purpose forms the roots from which all things come; your purpose becomes fulfilled by the blossoming of many branches into a fully mature tree.

Life-purpose statements are broad and large—all-encompassing of your unique light. You can sift through the rich details you have gathered together so far in your healing process for clues. For example, refer to the work you did in chapter 5, identifying some of your greatest joys and passions. Also—and this is a big one—go back to your "message in the mess" from chapter 2. All of these points of reference will help you to concisely define your life purpose.

I describe my life purpose this way: "I am an instrument of divine light and love." That is my overarching big statement. As we discussed earlier, Don Carlson's life purpose was "When people meet me, they leave feeling better than when they arrived."

Now it's your turn.

Draw your Tree of Life, labeling each branch with those passions or areas of life, or projects and people that fulfill your life's purpose. (Draw the extra branches that will be your future growth.) Please rewrite your life purpose statement at the base of the tree.

My life purpose is:

YOUR STORY IS YOUR GOLD

You are not alone in this time of change. The universe conspires on your behalf to help you heal and thrive. When you choose to let go of something that has been keeping you down, you are signaling to the universe—like a tuning fork drawing energy to yourself—that you are actively in partnership with all that is conspiring on your behalf so that you can bring your maximum gift home to the planet. All lights are on! You are ordinary but have become extraordinary in the wake of surviving the unthinkable heartbreak that ultimately opens you to grace and love, when you allow her to enfold you in her loving embrace.

Throughout the pages of this book so far, you have gone through a process of healing in which you have emptied out, and now you are ready to be filled. You have released many of your fears, doubts, anger, and tears, and the light is shining brightly from your eyes now. You have turned your loss into gold. Your holy grail is calling you toward your greatness, and it always will. It's an ideal that makes growth and change so exciting and motivating. However, your holy grail is simultaneously within your reach right now. You're really evolving into your life purpose now. And while you may not know exactly how it's going to manifest, you know that it's within you. The alchemy of change is the point on the journey when you are remembering why you came to earth. It's coming into focus.

Are you ready to see it, know it, and claim it?

STEPPING BACK INTO LIFE

There was a time in my life where I was in spiritual study and baffled by teachers who would say they could feel the life force of a tree. I could certainly see the tree, but I did not feel the tree as it was being a tree. I loved trees but was never a real tree hugger. As my husband's death breathed new life into me, I became very much aware of all surrounding life as I awakened to deeper feelings brought on by heartbreak. I had been heartbroken open to feeling all living things. During their epic *Power of Myth* dialogues, Joseph Campbell spoke of this broken-open love of life when he said to Bill Moyers, "Suddenly you're ripped out into being alive. And life is pain and life is suffering and life is horror, but by God, you're alive and it's spectacular."

It is in our darkest hour when we touch our pain and suffering that we can also make the connection to humanity. This inner connectedness to all living things is our awakening to all of life. This is the time when I became a tree hugger; I started hugging them all the time and blowing kisses to the clouds and noticing the medicine of the animals. My eyes opened up, and I saw everything that was alive at a time when I needed to. We don't have to wait until we transition from death to awaken to this feeling of returning to the divine source; it's a feeling that runs like a lightning rod up our spine, connecting us to that one heart and one light of the universe—connecting us to all things and all energies.

As you touch this point of suffering and you come back, you bring your gift with you; this is the alchemy of change where your purpose is revealed to you.

Three months before Richard died, we were coming up our big hill on foot, walking together, stride for stride, and holding hands. Richard turned to me to make sure as he spoke that I was really listening, and he said, "Kris, you know what I love about the human spirit? I love that there are people in this world who take their greatest tragedy and allow it to move them forward and add greater meaning to their lives." As he spoke these words, I knew he was thinking about a family who had lost their son to an accident with a drunk driver, and how the parents were forging ahead with a deeper purpose from their loss.

As I sat at our fireplace coming to terms with his death, just a few months later, these words came back to me, as clear as a bell tolls, and I knew the only way to honor Richard and our lives was to find my way to carry him forward with greater meaning and to inspire others in the process.

Some friends told me about a woman who had recently lost her husband and was suffering. I had just received the unbound galleys of my book *Heartbroken Open*. I told them to go ahead and introduce us, that I would be happy to meet with Mary. We met and shared a meal without wine; Mary was ten years into her sobriety. She shared her story of how she lost her husband, and as I listened, I reached across the table to hold her hand. She was so devastated and lost. I looked into her eyes and said, "Mary, you don't have to walk the widow's walk alone. I know it's not a club you wanted to belong to, but I'm here to usher you through. You have to trust someone, and I hope you see in my eyes a reflection of where you'll be if you trust me. You will transform and ascend from this time of grief."

I'm happy to say that Mary did follow my instructions—every letter. She is one of the most transformed women I know. She now meditates, practices yoga, and has become a world traveler. She is moving forward but is very sovereign as she does so. The best thing—Mary went through her dark night of the soul and stayed sober. I've never felt more proud, and I'm so honored that she allowed me to be her doula as she rebirthed a new life.

The best way to save yourself is to bend down and reach far to help somebody else out of the trenches. That's what sharing your story does. That's what leading my Heartbroken Open retreats did, opening my home to women who had lost their husbands through death and divorce. At first I thought I was the only woman in my forties who had lost my husband, and suddenly I had fifty women in my living room. I had this notion that most widows—just like the word "widows" sounds—are older. But, no, it turns out there is many a "willow" in the world (that's my term for a young widow!). There are men of all ages who lose their loves, too. In our circle of sharing, we made sure we allowed time for everyone in the room to tell their story, which is so healing, and the wisdom present from all was mind-blowing. I guarantee that every woman there chose to be the hero after being in that circle and hearing the stories and feeling the hearts of every woman. All present were living through different stages of their healing, but no matter where they were along their journey, it gave them courage and strength to know that they weren't walking alone.

One woman talked about how being there gave her permission to live again. Many of us can't imagine living on without the love of our life. But I am here to assure you that you are not living without the love of your life. You're only living without their physical presence. They are very much with you, and you carry them forward—especially with your history and your stories of them.

This past year marked the tenth anniversary of Richard's passing, and so much life had happened in the past ten years. I decided to hold a candlelight circle with many of our best friends and my family in the room. My grandkids were present: Caden was seven, Kayson five, and Kennedy three. Everyone held a candle and shared a lovely story and memory of Richard. At the end, Caden and Kayson, who had listened so intently, both claimed their grandfather with such love and pride. I cried, realizing they had just met the most special soul, their grandfather, through the eyes of everyone who loved him.

Today, at this stage of the journey, you understand your journey and why it happened the way it did. You're in the place of unfolding the meaning and connecting the dots. What has your suffering taught you? How has this changed you? How has it served you well? Most important—how will you serve others?

You now know why and how you're connected to humanity, and you're thinking about how you can give back to the world. When you think back on some of your darkest moments, you realize what sweet relief it is to be here—to feel your connection with humanity in your own way.

When I'm speaking at an event and ask a room full of people how many have *not* had their heart broken, usually no one raises their hand. On the rare occasion when someone does, I assume they must be a narcissist or completely numb, or perhaps they permanently live in an enlightened state. Truth is, we all go through forms of abuse, abandonment, neglect, and suffering at different times in our lives. We all have our hearts broken because we all love. Joy and suffering are our main ways of connecting—but more consistently we connect through our suffering. A wise teacher once said, "There is only one thing to do when the fear of losing something or someone you love comes up, and that is to love more."

Connecting to humanity through your story is one way to love more—to love big. Sharing our story becomes our legacy, and sharing stories of those we've lost is how they live on. We never tire of stories because they reveal and sometimes resolve the suffering that we all endure. The lessons of another can be your "Aha! The light goes on!" moment where one small insight can yield big life-changing results. There's so much healing that happens when we can realize that we are never suffering alone. At any given time, we are connected to others who are going through the same journey that we are, and that is so comforting. It is one of the great benefits of living in this time, with the web and social media. And your story is your own alchemical process of turning all of it—all of the heartache you can hardly believe you've survived—into gold.

Look around you now, at the landscape of your life. What is your safe place to land? Have you found your tribe of sojourners to support you in your process? More and more, your safe place is showing itself in the shape of a web of support and love—new friendships forming, old friendships ripening, and colleagues and collaborators popping up in surprising ways. You are supported by others while also becoming increasingly self-reliant. This web of love is essential to having the interdependence needed to imagine a new dream for your life. It is easy to be a victim who retreats from new connections in favor of isolation, but this web of support in which you've enrolled won't let you dally alone for long. *You must share your hero's journey with your circle of fellow sojourners.* This is the golden key to your deeper healing as you release your story to them so that you can receive the opening to a new chapter in your life. This is a very important step.

Throughout this book, you have been deep-diving into your soul—inquiring, probing, and listening intently to your innermost thoughtful Self. You have been writing a new story, a healing story based on your choice to be the hero. These are tools and structures for helping you to clarify your purpose and gather your inner warrior as you find and claim your holy grail. At this stage, you're getting crystal clear about who you want to reach with your story and why.

As for the *how*, there are so many ways to tell your story today that your imagination is practically your only limitation. You can become part of a Facebook group of like-minded souls and share your story with those you connect with there. You can write a book, a short story, a screenplay, or a stage play, or compose a song. You can start a podcast, develop a telecourse, lead a workshop, or train to be a therapist or coach who specializes in the aspect of life that you are becoming a master of. You can express what you have lived through the art you make, the food you prepare, or the quality of presence and love you bring to your work. You can share your story with just one person, when the opening arises naturally in conversation and as you are ready to do so. There are unlimited ways you can bring your story through the great arc of sharing.

The bottom line is that your way out of the dark woods of suffering and fully back into life is through what you choose to give back to humanity and how you decide it best serves to share your story.

Finally, at this stage, in order to feel free, you must accept the change that happened through heartbreak, and you must forgive yourself and the other who hurt you. The one who died. The one who left you. The one who wouldn't leave. The one who betrayed you. The one who was reckless with your heart. Or it may be that you need to forgive yourself for what you didn't do for someone else, or what you didn't do to care for yourself.

THE ULTIMATE DISCOVERY

You are the hero. There is no question about this anymore. Now you're living, more and more, from the place of giving back. While you recently knew yourself as a heartbroken person, you now have a new normal that involves discovering the joy of who you are.

The alchemy of change has begun to expose the true gift of this journey, one that will become even clearer in chapters 8 and 9. It's the ultimate discovery that your life belongs to you. And no matter what happens in it, you can always love life. If you can believe that and know it with every fiber of your being, then everything else you do in your life is secondary to the full-on adventure that is available to you. *My little kid inside squeals, "No matter what, I get to play!"*

Look at my friend Lisa. As of this writing, she had just finished chemotherapy five months earlier, facing death in the mirror, and yet she drove all the way up to the Bay Area from Los Angeles so we could enjoy each other's company as she transported me and my broken foot up to my Mount Shasta retreat. She chose to be the hero of her own story—a choice that continues to reveal her radiance, aliveness, and agelessness as she continues to deeply love the life that she has and her second chance to discover more.

This is what the alchemy of change is all about. It reveals you. It brings out into the light of day what is on the inside. It is the elixir that makes the unknown become known. The universe conspires on your behalf at this point. Opportunities are abundant, and you are totally in the flow of your life purpose. You are ready to serve.

We, your fellow heroes, cannot wait to find out what that life purpose is.

SOUL MANTRA:

Sit quietly and breathe for five minutes as you repeat:

I am in the flow of my life's purpose.
I am free to be me.

SOUL INQUIRY:
HOW CAN I EMBRACE CHANGE WITH EASE AND GRACE?

The process of change can be messy. Transition and change continually come into our lives, quickly bringing new waves of loss, transition, and confusion. Being intimate with your own process and asking yourself meaningful questions will help you to move with the flow of change.

1. How have I changed in this process of transformation?
2. What changes have taken place that I need to accept now so that I can move forward?
3. Who or what do I need to let go of in order to allow myself to change?
4. How can I create more peace within myself? In what part of my life do I need to remember the words "this too shall pass"?
5. What am I most grateful for?
6. What is my life purpose—my holy grail?

Your New Story • *transformational writing process*

Your story is your gold. Write about how your story is a reflection of your life purpose. What do you want to give? How do you want to serve? If you were going to post your story on your Facebook page today, sharing it with your community of friends and loved ones, what would you say?

_____

_____

_____

_____

_____

_____

_____

_____

Chapter 8

Rebirthing a New Life

> **The Promise of Chapter 8**—You will see how your heartbreak has created a new beginning for you. Forgiveness opens you to the miracles that await you. You are on your way to living your most vibrant life.

On December 28, 2008, just two years after Richard's transition, my daughters and I were traveling home from my parents' fiftieth wedding anniversary on a commuter flight from Eugene, Oregon, to San Francisco. We walked up to check our bags, and the attendant, a middle-aged Polynesian man, looked at our tickets and commented that the three of us weren't seated together. He then took it upon himself to rearrange our seats, saying that he felt strongly that we should be traveling together during the holidays. As we boarded our petite fifty-seater plane, the girls sat on my right across the aisle, leaving the window seat next to me open. A tall man stood in front of me, hunched over in the small cabin as he greeted me and asked to get to his seat next to mine at the window. The girls let out an odd giggle as he stood there, and I felt some stirrings that resembled butterflies in my gut. As I stood to allow him to pass, and then sat back down, my heart raced, and the strongest feeling came over me that I needed to speak to this man. I looked over and said, "Hello," but he only smiled and nodded as he pulled his laptop out, clearly not wanting to talk. I quieted down, leaving him his privacy.

On the descent of the flight, I was still feeling urged to speak to my fellow passenger as he began to put his laptop away. I asked him if it was a workday for him. He replied, "Oh, yes. I'm sorry. It is. I would have loved to have chatted with you, but I have a meeting this afternoon right after we land." As we talked further, we found we both had siblings in Eugene that we were visiting. He asked me if it was a workday for me—"I notice you have your laptop with you, as well."

"Not really, but I'm a writer," I replied.

He smiled. "Have you published anything I might know of?"

"You might be familiar with my late husband's work. Richard Carlson. He wrote *Don't Sweat the Small Stuff*," I responded.

He didn't say anything, so I looked over at him. He sat upright, looking straight ahead, but appeared visibly distraught and even had lost a little color.

I said, "What? Did you know Richard?" He shook his head as if in disbelief as he took a deep breath. I repeated, "*What?*"

He said, "Did he die on a flight to JFK a little over two years ago?"

I looked at him even closer now. "Yes. How did you know that he died going to JFK?"

He continued to shake his head as he said, "I was seated directly behind your husband on that flight. I was the first to assist the crew members and even helped lift him out of his seat."

I burst into tears.

"What are the odds of this happening, that we would be seated together and have this conversation?" I asked.

He replied, "There are no odds."

The man at the ticket counter. Divine grace. The girls giggling. My gut feelings. This meeting was unmistakably divinely orchestrated. I had been praying to meet someone who had been with Richard on the day he passed. Because I had not been there with him in his last moments on that flight, there was nothing I wanted more than to meet someone who had been. This marked the miracle that really helped me rebirth a new life.

About the same time, I could feel Richard's spirit. He had stayed so close to me these first years of grief, and now it was time for him to be moving along on his journey, rebirthing, too.

A friend once asked me why my life was full of serendipity but hers wasn't. My reply was that her life likely had just as many signs of providence but that perhaps she hadn't made that connection to the divine—she hadn't answered the call of spirit through her awareness and her deep belief within her agreement with reality. Being present is key so you don't miss the nuances of spirit when they appear.

Presence literally opens us to the divine and all of her guidance and mystery at the neurochemical level. It opens our reticular activating system (RAS), which is a set of interconnected nuclei at the base of the brain that is responsible for regulating wakefulness and the transitions between sleep and wakefulness. In essence, it is the gateway to our conscious awareness. In his book *Getting Things Done,* David Allen describes the role of awareness as the RAS on-switch: "Just like a computer, your brain has a search function—but it's even more phenomenal than a computer's. It seems to be programmed by what we focus on and, more primarily, what we identify with."

The hallmark of the divine cannot be missed unless you are simply unaware that she exists. She calls to you—through feeling and intuition, through "chance" encounters, through choices and decisions that present themselves to you. As you answer the call of the divine, so will you be guided into and through the mystery by her grace. You will discover, as I have, that life uses serendipity and synchronicity to lay down a path in front of you, showing you the way. Life will lead you, as it has always done all the days of your life. And it will require both your full participation and your deep surrender. You must allow the divine to come to you and through you.

When a child is born, the birthing process requires surrender, and so too does this form of rebirth. You are giving birth to the next evolution of yourself. *You are birthing a new life.*

It was a couple of days after the miracle meeting with the man on the plane who had held Richard's space during his transition, and I awoke for the first time ever on his side of the bed. The words rang loud and clear as I opened my eyes to the morning light.

"He didn't leave you, he died."

My heart whispered these words to me, and I woke up feeling different: I knew I was *out*. I was free to be me again. Many times I had wondered if I would ever wake up feeling myself again, yet grateful to have another day. But this day marked a new beginning for me. *I will never be the same. I am changed, but I am better. I am more me than I've ever been. And I love life more now, with deeper connection and a greater appreciation for all of it.* This is what I knew with complete certainty.

If only Richard knew me now. If only he could see the woman I am now. I am now all that he knew I could be. He saw my potential—and I know he fulfilled his.

You know that feeling after you've had the flu and you're suddenly hungry again—after you just wanted to die on the bathroom floor twelve hours earlier? When the cloak of grief falls, and you realize acceptance of your loss, it's a total feeling of renewal as you are born again and thirsty for more. This aliveness—this resurrection— is such a sweet part of the hero's journey. Allow it to be real by letting yourself *feel* it. Allow yourself to have a complete celebration of this new beginning. And allow the guidance of the divine as you feel your way into your new life.

COMING BACK TO LIFE

Surprisingly, we think coming back to life means we are out of the dark woods and into the light of the meadow where we will forever be in joy, exuberantly alive! The child within us, the part of us that is innocent and idealistic, sees no reason why this can't be the way it is all of the time. Truth is, we will visit the wilderness many times over, and walk deep into the forest, through valleys and scaling mountains to climb higher. And we will continue to journey and rebirth—coming back to more life every time. As you are now "rebirthed," please be gentle with the new you. You are like a newborn fawn stepping on wobbly legs. Please tread carefully along as you see life with new eyes. Your perspective has broadened. You can see the bigger picture now.

In a recent workshop, where I was leading a group of women through a transformational weekend, we entered the dark woods together, trusting the heart and humanity of one another as we revealed secrets that had been hidden in the shadows. I was surprised by how much each of the leader-participants in the room carried shame and guilt for her past choices. Yet the tears, the screams of agony, were a release of shame, guilt, regret, and other emotions that had been pushed down or painted over with a new image and identity.

Many of the things we human beings do are innocent acts—not as reckless or devious as we may think at first glance. For example, one woman who spoke out had come from Iran. She was carrying the shame of having had an abortion, but it was compounded terribly because she was actually carrying the shame of an entire nation on her back—a country where it was so unacceptable to choose abortion. As she spoke up, many women in the room related to her pain and anguish and joined her in giving voice to it.

That's not to say there isn't evil in the world that is well thought-out and intentional. But I could clearly see that there was no evil in this room. There were people with good intentions who had innocently made errors in judgment that caused themselves or someone else to suffer, and they still carried the guilt. But these are good people driven to do good works in the world—driven to make the world a better place. Do you think that they can do their work better without carrying a ten-thousand-pound sack of stones on their backs equal to the guilt they feel?

The deeds that are done cannot be undone, but they can drive you forward to embrace what is good, as long as you forgive yourself. Letting go of shame and guilt frees you to be yourself and shine your light bigger and brighter, and it comes through forgiving those things that you did at a time in your life when you didn't know better. Those were choices you made then, but you have learned that you would choose differently now. You are a new person today, one who no longer has to pretend to be anyone or anything other than who you are. That was another life; doesn't it feel that way?

What does it mean to be free of that encumbrance? Your ego talked you into believing things about yourself that have nothing to do with who you are. Circumstances show up for you to break through that illusion—circumstances that flush out fear to the surface by discrediting you, humiliating you, or otherwise holding your feet to the fire—

and you step further into yourself and a deeper understanding of who you are in your essence, in your being, not who you used to want people to think you are.

I was speaking to a friend who was going through a divorce. "I'm worried. This divorce is so ugly and bitter. I'm afraid I'll lose all my friends," he admitted. I said, "Your true friends know who you are. You're getting bigger, and your smaller friends will fall away. You'll attract new people who match you now. It's OK. You can let go of the people who leave." In a year's time, he had three new friends who were living their lives in a much more elevated way—in how they were doing business, finance, relationships, and personal development.

As a part of the soul's path of growth, which includes the journey into and back out of the shadow, each of us has put on a cloak to conceal the aspects of ourselves that we could not or would not accept—for reasons that are unique to each person. Most often put on unconsciously, the cloak becomes a shield and hides the thoughts, feelings, and behaviors that we believed would make us unlovable or unworthy. This is the shadow. In actuality, it's not a monster or the boogeyman under the bed. It's the rejected, unwanted, or disowned parts of who we naturally are. In that sense, the shadow is our sacred ally, holding the many parts of us, both dark and light, until we're able to consciously reclaim them—until we are ready to be whole again.

What we discover upon facing the shadow self and embracing those aspects that we deem shameful or less lovable is the relief and empowerment that come from owning the totality of ourselves. When we remove the cloak and the burden of hiding, we're actually getting larger as our light shines brighter; we discover that we're more than, not less than. We're becoming weightless and freer as we authentically express who we are.

It's true that once you awaken you will never go fully back to sleep, but even the modern-day mystics and transformational leaders, I know, go through their times of coming out into the world and then retreating back inward to the wilderness of the unknown. This back-and-forth movement between our inner and outer worlds, as we discussed in the previous chapter, is crucial for the process of healing and transformation—and for rebirthing a new life. Like a snake that sheds its skin, you will rebirth many times. We need to take ourselves away from the world from time to time so that we can reconnect within and without. *What do I need? What must I give to myself that I've been demanding from someone else? What kind of support do I need from others that I'm not asking for? What beliefs am I holding that are perpetuating fear? What choices have I made that are limiting me? How can I transform this fear into excitement for the adventure?* These are just some of the kinds of questions that it's easier to hear the answers to when we retreat from the noise of daily life. Retreating inward, we become more intimate and honest with ourselves. Returning again to the world, we meet life with greater availability and presence.

We are all the human catastrophe and the masterpiece. Each of us embodies all the colors of a glorious tapestry woven together to portray the story of our life. We can be hedonists, and we can be monks. We can be dictators, and we can be leaders. We can be lovers one day and haters the next. We can master, and we can fall.

What are you missing if you deny yourself your real and true thoughts and feelings? What are you missing if you don't heed the call of spirit making that connection to the divine?

Sitting across from another friend at dinner, I was speaking about a retreat that I had just led. Sharing with him about some of the things that happen in a transformational circle, I talked about anger work. He exclaimed, "Oh, anger. I don't like anger. I wouldn't like that." I'm sure I raised my eyebrows a little and said, "Ohhh? You don't like

anger?" Knowing that this was his repressed shadow, and that it probably leads him to be passive-aggressive when he does feel anger, I pressed forward a bit. "So, you don't think you ever feel anger, *really?*" Then he innocently and endearingly replied, "Well, the other day, I felt my chest tighten as my mother was going on and on over the phone about how she was feeling. I think I may have felt anger because my mom never ever listened to me, and here I was listening to her." Aha, there it was. The shadow was out in plain view, and it was a recognition and release—and nothing to be afraid of, only acknowledged enough to see it and let go.

The meditation master Osho said, "If we all lived our lives as an open book, there would be nothing to hide." There would be no more shame. As we embrace all of those aspects of Self that we don't want to be, or that we don't want others to see, we become fully embodied and fully expressed, and moreover we stop acting out on those hidden insecurities and demons that have been given too much energy in secrecy.

What then? What does a fully embodied and fully expressed life look like? What does it feel like? The answers require vision, the ability to reach with your imagination and heart toward the life you deeply want to give birth to.

Marcia Wieder, the renowned author and founder of Dream University, invited me to her last live coaches training in the spring of 2014. At the event, she asked us: "What is your dream for your future?" Much to my surprise, I drew a blank. I realized in that moment that I hadn't been dreaming or visioning. Up to that point in my own process of grieving and healing, I hadn't been able to let go of the life I had. I felt quite at home in the present, but I hadn't dreamed about building a future. That's when I knew what I had to do next if I was going to birth a new life . . . a new dream.

I had to let go of the life I had known and loved for so long; I was called to step into a new one.

LETTING GO—CLEARING THE PATH
TO YOUR NEW LIFE

Whatever has happened to you, you've accepted this loss now. You have lived, loved, and gone through the process of healing, and are no longer in question about how this has changed you. You know. And you are in it. You have evolved into this new being. And it has come from a death—whether literal or figurative. Someone died or something ended or some aspect of your innocence is gone. Now, in order to birth your new dream and move into wholeness, you have to let it all go. "Live, Love, Let Go" is the mantra of rebirth.

Are You Stuck? Preparations for Letting Go

In the previous chapter, when I described how grace had swept in and blown open the doors of my perception when I was in great pain, I explained that I knew I could have gotten stuck in a place of terrible despair that would have sent my life in a direction that I don't want to go in. We often talk about "feeling stuck" or "being stuck" in a casual way, like getting the heel of your shoe temporarily caught in a crack in a sidewalk. In reality, being stuck can have devastating repercussions. Months and years can evaporate while we miss out on all kinds of opportunities—for love and connection, for fun and adventure, for work and financial abundance, for creative collaborations that can make a difference in the world. We can miss out on fulfilling our potential and living our purpose!

Let's not settle for that.

But first, how do you know when you're stuck? When you don't do things differently. When you feel uninspired. When you don't take risks. When you only do what feels familiar and safe. When you feel tied to your life, believing that your options and choices are limited.

When you feel like you're living inside a glass dome (think snow globe), and you kind of like it that way. You can see everything happening outside of your dome, but you want to remain inside, where it feels safe. Other signs of being stuck include various levels of anxiety, depression, or addiction, or having a lot of conflict to contend with in your life (conflict can sometimes masquerade as the aliveness that we're really longing for).

Don't worry, though! This too shall pass. Whether you've been in a holding pattern for two months, two years, or twenty years, you can choose to resume forward motion now, at this stage of your hero's journey. Throughout this process, you have been leaning into the fears at the root of why you sometimes hold on to the past, whether consciously or unconsciously. You've emerged through your hoops of fire and embraced change in an empowered way. The next big step is one of letting go so that you are free to imagine and step into your new life.

Letting go in this context means releasing whatever is tethering you to the past. This could be stories, behaviors, activities, beliefs, attitudes, or feelings that are no longer good for you. As you take this next step, you are leaving the "waiting room" and entering fully into your life. Now it's time to empty out so that you can be filled up anew—with new thoughts and feelings, new inspirations and ideas, new opportunities, a new vision for your life.

At my group retreats, we do a simple letting-go process that changes people's lives. We bear witness to what each person wants to release and what they want to open the doors to receiving. After an evening session of sharing and writing, we come together in a circle in the morning to support each other in letting go of anything that is holding us back. There is tremendous strength derived from the group's assurance that "you can do this"—you can be free of anything that has you mired and unable to move ahead. In the writing of this book, it's my hope that some of the courage, willingness, and good humor of these remarkable individuals is transmitted here on the page—to support you in knowing that you can do it, too.

To begin, take out your journal and pen, and if you can, light a candle. You may even want to play some beautiful music at a soft volume, to invite and welcome your feelings as you answer the following questions:

THE LETTING-GO PROCESS

- *What do you need to let go of in order to put yourself at the starting place of something new and begin opening up to that?*

- *Is there an emotion or feeling state that you need to let go of? Is it self-pity, jealousy, guilt, loneliness, unworthiness, hurt, anger, or bitterness?*

- *Is there a pattern of thought that you need to let go of? Is it blame, regret, feeling overwhelmed, worry and anxiety, overthinking, fear of failure, or fear of "ending up alone"?*

- *Is there a limiting belief that is keeping you stuck that you would be willing to release? Do you believe you're not good enough, smart enough, hot enough, or rich enough? Do you believe you're never going to change?*

- *Are you caught in a behavior pattern that's getting in the way of change? Are you chronically overworking, overeating, overspending, isolating, or otherwise neglecting your well-being?*

- *Do you need to let go of a relationship or a way of being inside of a particular relationship?*

- *Do you need to let go of a job or a way of doing your job that no longer serves you?*

- *Is there an aspect of your self-image or identity that you need to let go of at this stage of your hero's journey?*

- *Do you need to let go of a long-held dream so that you can create a new dream?*
- *Now write a letter of letting go. Without censoring yourself, proclaim something specific that you are ready to release. One big let-go at a time is best. Address your letter in whatever way feels right to you—writing it to yourself, another person, a guardian angel, the Universe, or to someone or something else.*
- *Allow a day to pass, and then release your letter to the elements of nature. Burn it in a fire (safely). Release it to the sea. Or scatter it to the wind. As you do this, repeat the words:* I surrender. I release. I let go to the elements to receive. *And so it is.*

THE RETURN OF VISION AND LIGHT

Although we must accept that periods of navigating the wilderness, where the path is untrodden, is a part of the hero's journey, we can't live in the wilderness our whole life. We have to come out of the wilderness of personal growth. You go in and gather your wisdom, your knowledge, then bring it out into the world and share it. This book is that for me. It's the result of doing that and waiting for the moment when it wanted to be birthed. There was a completion to the process at the ten-year mark that opened me to the possibility of this work coming through me. The gift is that I can shorten the time and energy it takes for other people. I can shorten their duration in the dark woods and accelerate their movement back to life.

That's what the hero is willing to do—for as long as it takes, until that alchemical process takes place. Suddenly it's there: to be written, to be spoken, to be shared in whatever way you wish. You can't even shut it off. You can't stop it. In the creative sense, your water has broken and the "baby" is coming.

You can ignore your gifts for a while, but the light of who you are can't be shut off, either. Despite the fact that people have called me "Sunshine" my whole life, it took me a long time to own my light and my purpose for being here.

Which brings me back to the day I met George Clooney . . .

It was my celebration and rite of passage of turning forty. Richard had given me an amazing choice: A new car or a first-class trip to Italy for my birthday. I thought a new car would make it look like I was in a midlife crisis, and I am so glad I chose Italy—and a wonderful, truly beautiful honeymoon it was for us. My goddaughter was being christened on my birthday, and I joked around with Lisa, who had sold her family villa on Lake Como to George Clooney, that I wanted to meet him and that's what she should give me for my birthday gift. So she scheduled the christening in the small chapel above George's house and asked him if he would open the house for a reception. George was so delightful, and he stayed around and chatted with us. But it was the moments before meeting George that took my breath away. I was sitting in the church when I had an experience. It was a deep understanding of the pain and suffering of Jesus as I was mesmerized by the figure on the cross that hung in front of me. I felt so much love and light. As I was having this experience, Richard was standing at the entrance to the church, and he took a photo that shows glorious and enormous rays of light streaming from my head and shoulders and around my body, reaching all the way to the mural of Christ. Nowhere else in the dimly lit and cavernous space was there a source of light. My first thought was that it must have been a visual phenomenon caused by light streaming in through the church windows. But as Lisa and I pored over the christening photos, months later, she reminded me that there weren't any windows in this church.

Three years before Richard died, he took a picture that is a visual

have been holding on to, place value on each stone or twig as you lay them out in front of you. This may seem silly at first, but speak aloud to each one, saying what you need to say to the person (who is now represented by twig or stone or leaf) you have harbored anger and resentment toward or who you feel has wronged you in some way. When you are finished, cover that object with a large leaf, tying it closed with a piece of raffia or twine.

As you complete this task, as many times as you need to, dig a hole in the ground and bury your object, covering it with the earth. If you are near water, prepare the same way, but release the object to the sea, stream, or lake. As you bury or release the object, repeat the following statement:

I leave this anger, this resentment, this pain here to Mother Earth to nurture and seed her love. I no longer need to hold on to this. I forgive you, I forgive me, and I release what no longer serves me. I am free.

A Course in Miracles says, "Forgiveness is the healing of the perception of separation." As you move from heartbreak to wholeness, you gradually remember that you are never separate and alone. And you discover that forgiveness opens the door to whatever miracles you are seeking to help bring you the rest of the way home.

SOUL MANTRA 1:

Close your eyes, sit comfortably, and breathe deeply.
Repeat the mantra:

I live. I love. I let go.

SOUL MANTRA 2:

Close your eyes, sit comfortably, and repeat the mantra:

I am here now. I am present for miracles to flow into my life.

THE SOUL INQUIRY:
PRESENT-MOMENT LIVING AND MIRACLES

Chaos has ended, and you are approaching life with calm clarity. Life is beginning to stabilize. The fire has reseeded the forest with new possibilities. You can accept your life exactly as it is. You have lived, you have loved, and you are ready to let go and experience the miracles that are present for you.

Please pull out your journal and answer the following questions.

1. How do I see balance and harmony coming back to my life?
2. Am I spending enough time in nature—in stillness—so I can become more present in my life?
3. What have I let go of? How will letting go of the past impact my life?
4. How will forgiveness change my life?
5. In what ways am I free now?

Your New Story • *transformational writing process*

Your new life has begun. Write your rebirth story. What does your fully embodied and fully expressed life look like? What does it feel like? What are you doing? Who are you being? How does divine guidance show up in your life?

_____

_____

_____

_____

_____

_____

_____

_____

Chapter 9

Into Wholeness, Returning to Joy

The Promise of Chapter 9—You are now feeling a sense of completion and celebrating the integration of all that you have learned. You will see how you are a sovereign unfolding into wholeness as you return to joy! You are the hero who will inspire others.

When Richard died, my fear was that he was gone to me. But then I could feel him as if he were standing in the room or lying beside me. I suddenly knew that I was with him and he was with me in the most delicious way because our hearts were together as one. I could feel his bliss in the divine. I'll never forget realizing that he was now my deeper connection to the divine as I straddled universes in those early days of transition. There were days I felt blissed out by feeling Richard's essence, so wonderfully delighted as he danced in the light of spirit, and he brought his light back to me.

I had no idea that I would embark on my heroine's journey with this deeper call into the abyss, into the divine. This was the event that would catalyze my return to wholeness. It was this deep feeling and understanding that gave me the strength and peace to move forward and step into the journey—and heed the call of my soul to share my message through my story.

But those nourishing waves of connection gradually receded from the shore of my awareness. I got busy, like everyone else. Sometimes we lose the intensity of those connections simply because we become more grounded in the world, in this dimension. Even though the veil has come down, for a time, it's easy to lose our ability to be present to that deeper conversation that is always happening within us below the surface of our busyness. Beyond the ego and all the self-talk, beyond all of our fears and heartbreaks, under the surface of loss is a palpable wonderment that is just waiting to be probed and mysteriously explored.

People talk about having a wanderlust, a sacred restlessness that takes them to the road of travels. But what are we restless for? It's not a longing that is likely to be met by going to a yoga retreat or even embarking on an adventure trip to a far-flung place (although those are excellent things to do). There is a desire sourced from our souls that is more aptly described as a *wonderlust*. Wonderlust is about being able to see beyond the physical, beyond form, into the hidden beauty of this catalyst of change that has come through this experience. This time of wonder is a time of awakening to all of life— awakening to a deep love affair with your life and all that's available in it. Especially to those pieces you've been quietly asleep to. It's time to wake up and lust for more.

Fear has a way of tying up so much time and energy, and blocking so much curiosity and inspiration, that you can feel completely estranged from the sheer miracle of being—a miracle that is only made sweeter with every breath and every beat of your heart. Fear of being alone is one of the blocks that comes with this package of being human. Early on, it was so clear to me that this was one of my greatest fears, as it is for many. It was as if the clock had turned back time, and I was thrust back to the eighteen-year-old girl I was when I met Richard, and all of her insecurities bubbled up—the ones that had been hidden under the shield of Richard's light and love. The biggest one was the fear of being alone, because, of course, I hadn't felt that one in twenty-five years. Saturday night would come around, our date night, and I remember thinking, *Shit, I don't want to be alone on Saturday night.* I learned to call on my friends when this dread would rise up. Sometimes they would call on me first, sensitively anticipating my brokenhearted apprehension. Our dear friends Joe and Michael Bailey—Joe being Richard's coauthor for the book *Slowing Down to the Speed of Life*—had become great mentors, along with my other friends who held space for me and became my support. It was Joe and Michael who said, "There will come a day when you find a space within where you will enjoy your own company without your ego taunting you, insisting that you're going to be alone for the rest of your days." There will come a day when your real return to wholeness will be evident in your deeper connection to spirit and the divine guidance that never leaves you alone.

A little at a time, I came to understand that becoming a whole person meant not only facing my fear of being alone (a fear that was always present but masked by love)—and facing that fear over and over again—but getting to where I loved my time alone as I opened my heart to offering myself love and deeply engaging in the beauty of my experience, one that became more and more divine. I awakened to the life that is all around me to partake in an abundant feast of beauty. Over the past few years, I've realized that I really *do* love my own company. Moreover, I love *life*! The whole adventure of it. Every juicy bit.

This love of life, as I've hinted at throughout these pages, is the deepest healer of the human heart. Every day, we open our eyes to new possibilities and new opportunities. We get to love and be loved again. From mourning our losses, we inevitably awaken to a new dawn in our lives, where the sun rises again—warming us after a time of being frozen in fear and pain and chilled by uncertainty. The thaw happens even faster in those moments when we're aware of the breathtaking gift of being human in all of our fragility. We have this opportunity to be here on this earth now, at this time, breathing in love and exhaling fear. In a universe of infinite potentials, this is where we find ourselves. Right here. Awake. And hopeful about tomorrow. The wondrous nature of this fact has inspired countless innovations, love sonnets, and works of art. The twentieth-century novelist Franz Kafka wrote beautifully of life's constant readiness to embrace us, any time we are ready to simply open our arms:

> *You do not need to leave your room. Remain sitting at your table and listen. Do not even listen, simply wait, be quiet, still and solitary. The world will freely offer itself to you to be unmasked, it has no choice, it will roll in ecstasy at your feet.*

No matter what circumstances come our way, it's all a part of that greater love affair that serves us with this experience. Everything happens for us so that we may grow and evolve into our greatness. Just as we deepen our relationships with others through conversation and interactions, we deepen our relationship with life in the same ways. We have a constant flow of interplay, situations, and circumstances that help us see into our life experience with insight and understanding. In time, wisdom, vulnerability, and receptivity are born. These qualities sound soft at first, but they are the qualities of being (feminine qualities) that give us the greatest strength and resilience along our hero's path. Just as we become intimate with others, we become intimate with life, having this inner conversation that appreciates with deep wonder and utter gratitude all that is present.

As in the Japanese art of kintsugi, through care, attention, and intention, the broken pieces of us come together again, glued together by golden streams of feeling, forgiveness, gratitude, and grace. Through loving life and being loved by life, we are made whole again.

What Does Wholeness Look Like?

The idea of "wholeness" conjures up many ideas for many people, and so I ask you to have an open mind for the conversation. Across the many religious and spiritual texts, wholeness has many connotations and meanings. Because I'm passionate about using terms that don't separate us, I define wholeness as coming home in yourself, fully integrated and balanced as a sovereign person who places the love of life itself as the highest value and who is in service to the divine, giving of yourself in ways that you are authentically moved to. I do my best in my work to use terms that are more universally applicable; that's why I speak of "divine love," the supreme energy of spirit available to all. Rather than referring to God as innately masculine or feminine, I refer to "source" in a genderless way because God is divinely both and within all. Similarly, when I refer to the divine feminine and masculine energies of an individual, I am simply addressing those aspects of the divine that show up in the qualities of our humanness as energy takes form through our actions. The integration of these masculine and feminine qualities, as we'll be discussing in this chapter, is an important part of the return to wholeness.

If you are of a particular faith or spiritual tradition that doesn't identify with the idea of divine feminine and masculine, another way to approach wholeness is as the central and unifying relationship you have with Christ or God and how that plays out in your life every day.

Whatever our religious or spiritual traditions may be, I believe that we are all created in God's likeness, light beings made from Love. And we are born with a path to walk that is our own. As sovereign beings—women and men who are self-determining, unconditionally free, and possessing internal power that requires approval from no one—we get to choose how we navigate the journey. The life-changing choice we can all make is to be the hero and heroine in all circumstances, both those of joy and those of sorrow, as we choose love.

The divine order of things is promising when you love life in this wonderlust way. Rather than fateful thinking, faith and hope are dynamically alive when you love life. You are tuned in to your prayers of thanks. You are available to inspire others. And you offer yourself to the service of spirit and being led as a divine instrument . . . becoming the hands and feet, the ears, the eyes, the voice, and the one heart of God.

YOUR SACRED AGREEMENT WITH LIFE

In returning to your natural state of wholeness, fear falls away, replaced by a sense of completeness. You are in deep relationship with all living things while simultaneously independent and self-governing. With this comes great freedom of expression, clarity of purpose, and a deeper engagement. You see the bigger plan for your life. You connect the dots. You can see that something great has come from all you have experienced—and that it's leading you somewhere even greater.

Nothing you have been through, not even the darkest moments, is without a profound purpose. As your broken heart is healed and whole again, you are ready to remember why you came to earth.

Caroline Myss brought beautiful insight and understanding to what it means to honor our sacred agreement with the divine in her book *Sacred Contracts: Awakening Your Divine Potential*. She makes the stirring point that the great masters—Moses, Muhammad, Jesus, the Buddha—were not born enlightened. All had to awaken to the fullness of their sacred pledge and bond with life. Their life paths were not any more obvious to them than ours are to us. They had to learn to have faith and surrender their personal will to the divine and allow spirit to reveal the next steps on the journey. Each had to answer the call of spirit and connect to the divine, and they all experienced trials and tribulations requiring tenacity, strength, and faith to stay the course in trust.

Likewise, each of us has a divine purpose—a calling that is the expression of our greatest potential and therefore divinely inspired. In the fulfillment of our agreement with the divine, we meet people with whom we have sacred contracts. They help to usher us into our unique purpose by their presence in our lives, but also when they are no longer physically present. Sometimes that is the deepest way we serve one another—the greatest gift of love happens from the loss of love. In their absence, one of the many profound gifts these soul companions give to us, as we are broken open, is the opportunity to discover and reclaim aspects of ourselves that we have been estranged from, therefore operating on less than our full power. In the peaks and valleys of living life together, these are the people who show us, often unconsciously, the parts of ourselves we need to retrieve in order to be whole again.

Love serves us extremely well in this way.

What is required of us to fulfill our sacred agreement includes reclaiming the masculine and feminine aspects of ourselves that have been denied or disowned, just as we addressed with the shadow. We must embrace the deep responsibility to do this work of integration, to own all of who we are.

BEYOND GENDER IDENTITY—THE DIVINE MASCULINE AND FEMININE

Regardless of our gender at birth, both the masculine and feminine qualities are integral to who we are. We are born balanced and whole, male or female. If you think about it, for this short period in our infancy, we are quite androgynous until our identity is formed and we take on the cultural norms of what it means to be a "boy" and what it means to be a "girl." As infants, we don't care much about our gender. We are nurtured into our understanding of what it means to be masculine and feminine by our association with all that we see and touch, from the colors we wear to the toys we play with to the role models we are surrounded by. Mostly, we learn that our body parts are different and that they define our gender. Sure, our hormones also play a huge role in how we develop these masculine and feminine characteristics and the roles we adopt later as we grow into men and women. But I think we're too quick to leave these distinctions unquestioned. While we are beings born of a gender, I love that there is a new conversation about gender that the millennials, as a generation, are insisting on. Not willing to settle for being identified as anything but *human*—bristling at any label or categorization that degrades their innate wholeness—they have created the term "gender neutral." They are right in proclaiming that we can be all things, both masculine and feminine, and we don't need to be defined by any one aspect. In fact, I like to think of the highest male and female being balanced in the yin and yang qualities, those that would make a man of heart and a woman to be reckoned with!

For purposes of this conversation, let's spend a moment defining what's masculine and what's feminine in nature. Typically, we think of the high-testosterone alpha male as being dominant, linear, structured, and powerful in his physical body—the hunter, ready to provide and do battle. The feminine is considered soft, receptive, fluid, and open. Feminine beings are the gatherers and nurturers, holders of beauty and caretakers of wisdom who are high in intuition and emotional intelligence. They are able to make order of chaos, sit in the eye of the storm and create peace, and make scrambled eggs at the same time! In *The Book of Doing and Being,* author and filmmaker Barnet Bain takes a practical yet soulful approach to describing the dance of masculine and feminine qualities within each of us. In men, women, nonbinary, and transgender people alike, creativity and innovation are born within us when the dynamic qualities of will and action (masculine energies) come together with the receptive qualities of imagination, feeling, and being (feminine energies). When any of those aspects are repressed, abandoned, or relegated to the care of someone else, we experience a loss of power, to one degree or another. In relationship, and especially when we are separated from any of these elemental parts of ourselves, it's easy to innocently defer aspects of what it means to be masculine and feminine to each other.

I celebrate and embrace the divine feminine nature within every one of us, with all its chaos and mystery. The whirlpool and spiral of existence is the feminine way, and I love to swim and play in its undulations. It feels natural to me to approach daily life with my senses, feelings, and creativity fully engaged. But along my journey, I realized there were ways I had been incomplete in my masculine skills, and I equally celebrate the archetypal masculine energies. While many worldly successful women deny their feminine, I had lived a life with a man of heart who was very balanced in his masculine and feminine. I always said that in our home there were two mothers. Richard was the great protector, provider, and wholly discerning masculine leader, but he was equally nurturing, a man of heart. His being was fully integrated and his ego low at the time of his death. Two weeks before Richard had his pulmonary embolism, he was asked to do a local book signing in San Francisco for his latest book, *Don't Get Scrooged*. It happened on a Sunday, and I asked him if he'd like me to go along with him. He smiled and said, "No, it's fine. I'm not sure how well it's been promoted. I'll just go and be back by dinner." He walked out the door in a happy mood, and he walked back in, hours later, the same way. I gave him a kiss as he walked into the kitchen and asked him how it went. He replied, "It was perfect." I said, "Oh, good turnout?" He genuinely smiled and said, "No. It was a terrible turnout—not a single person showed, and I had a wonderful day anyway." I searched his face to see if he was for real, and he was. He was unaffected by a botched book signing. I knew the kind of ego that usually causes most of us so much suffering was practically nonexistent in Richard. He had passed his spiritual graduation test, and he transitioned two weeks later.

In our lives together, as I've said, Richard held the space of being a hunter and great provider but was also extremely kind, emotionally intelligent, and nurturing. He could live in spontaneity and fluidity but could also hold structure as a planner. In my innocence, as he held space for me to be fully embodied in the feminine, I deferred the masculine to my husband. I took for granted the feelings of protection his presence gave us and his high level of discernment in leading our family. Now that he was gone, I had to learn how to be the one in charge of protection in many ways, and I began to learn how to be discerning, too—at great cost.

My jagged edge of growth involved more than the cyber stalker

I described in chapter 4. Other men who came into my life after Richard's death, and all whom I trusted, saw a vulnerability that I did not feel and turned out to be looking to take advantage of me to benefit themselves. A newly hired assistant took advantage of my trust. A business and life adviser manipulated me into a loan for a large sum of money, which he has since defaulted on. Both of these men took advantage of my open and trusting nature, knowing my husband had overseen these aspects of our lives. The holes in my energy field were obvious, looking back, but at the time I was blind to the ways I lacked discernment, and I was vulnerable to male dominance in ways I could not recognize in my grief. In effect, I had been outsourcing to others certain attributes and strengths that are essential pieces of me—qualities and abilities that I needed to have ready access to; qualities that would be exercised to complete those missing parts of myself and bring me into balance to become the best version of myself. Yes, they were costly lessons and part of what my soul called in to teach me. I had to learn how to integrate and channel a different kind of energy that had always been part of my husband's gentle but powerful way. I had to call in the masculine energy of protecting myself and my family and make a commitment to myself to integrate my newfound masculine aspects into my awakening.

It is very clear to me that each of my initiations happened to allow me full integration of the masculine with my feminine qualities in order to bring all aspects and energies into harmony. As I progressed along my healing journey, I found myself wanting to take a quantum leap toward wholeness. This desire led me down a fascinating new road.

Every year, I choose an intensive training or workshop to participate in. I believe we never stop being students, and personal growth has always been my joy. I have long been interested in Carl Jung's approach to archetypes and in Joseph Campbell's work showing how the mythical journey of the hero is within us at the DNA level. Like these, Jean Shinoda Bolen's book *Goddesses in Everywoman* and Caroline Myss's work, as stated earlier, show us how to see energies that have become integrated into our collective consciousness through the awareness of and associations with mythical archetypes that are used for transformation. The idea is that each of us has embraced some archetypal traits more strongly in our being and way through life than others. When I entered into the yearlong 13 Moon process, it became a celebration of the 13 faces of the divine feminine that I could see embrace both masculine and feminine energies. (While mostly women enter this circle, on rare occasions men study the 13 Moons, too.) I had no idea that it would not only show me what I had lived and taught from the feminine parts of myself in my work with Heartbroken Open, but it would also help me embrace and strengthen the more fierce feminine energies as I stood up against the stalker. The 13 Moon circle I studied was developed by Ariel Spilsbury, who represents to me a divine example of the Great Mother and a wise woman in her crone years. I first met Ariel through my friend Christine Arylo, who has studied with Ariel.

Ariel had a fairy cottage I would visit now and again. As I walked up through the trees into the cottage in the woods that first time, I felt like I was entering a womb. When she opened her door, her light shone brightly from her crone-silver hair and her forget-me-not-blue eyes. The warmth of her love was so enticing and unconditional, I felt enfolded in her hug, a babe in my mother's arms again. The warmth of this God-Mother to all is not of this world—more etheric and angelic than girl-next-door. I sensed that I was about to have a wild experience.

Ariel invited me to sit in open-eyed meditation with her, and as

I did so, the room dissolved into a film of gold, and I had the feeling of floating as she began to shape-shift into a lion of kindness. At the end of our lovely hour, when I described to her what I saw, she said, with her deep fairy laugh adorning her words, "Well, of course, my dear. My name, Ariel, means 'heart of a lion.'"

As we talked further, I shared with her that when I received the beautiful goddess kit she had mailed me, which includes a feminine archetype card deck, there was one card missing. It was the "Initiator" card that has her image on it. She laughed out loud again, exclaiming, "Well, isn't she funny?" I asked who "she" was. "She" is the divine feminine *Great* Mother, the one who is considered the ultimate of nurturers.

Ariel had been asking the Great Mother what She had in store for her in her retirement, and here I was, asking her to hold another circle of the 13 Moons. It seems that She was more in favor of Ariel's "refirement" than her winding down as a teacher and mentor. I saw it as a unique opportunity to spend a year deeply immersed in the divine feminine and learning from the wellspring of Ariel's lineage in archetypal mythology, which includes visionaries such as Carl Jung, Joseph Campbell, and Jean Houston. And so she did it—Ariel refired up and held a group of us in a magical year of awakening. As she did this, she also realized that she needed to train leaders to carry on her work.

There were thirteen moons, thirteen circles, thirteen participants, and thirteen archetypes that we embodied fully in this yearlong process that stitched me together from a patchwork quilt into a golden tapestry of beauty. Starting on the new moon, we were taken back to the mists of Avalon, in a circle with twelve other goddesses all in training to become High Priestesses. Several of my colleagues had received this training in their personal development as leaders, so I understood that it would be an intense process—with alchemical changes that would allow us to shine brightly as the peacock in our initiation. We embraced and celebrated the thirteen archetypes on the new moon of each month:

The Great Mother
The Goddess of Compassion
The Priestess
The Creator/Destroyer
The Lady of Communion
The Muse
The Goddess of Love
The Primal Goddess
The Initiator
The Wise Woman
The Weaver/Dreamer
The Queen of Death
The Alchemical Goddess

When our circle came to a close, I emerged with a greater understanding of all the feminine energies I could access from this process. I emerged feeling fully embodied with grace. I birthed the fullness of the feminine in her magnificent wonder, and in her ability to graciously stand on her own—independent and sovereign and ready to transform my new strength into wholeness. While a 13 Moon circle might not be your ideal workshop, there are many other resources and ways you can choose to celebrate and discover the feminine and masculine archetypes and to learn how they play out in the quality of your journey as energies to be transformed.

This same archetypal celebration quality of group transformation exists for men, too. One of the most substantive bodies of work I know of for men is the ManKind Project, a global network of trainings and men's groups that was founded in the mid-1980s by Rich Tosi, Bill Kauth, and Ron Hering. One of their primary goals as a group is to help each other find their mission in life and explore the shadow that keeps them from living their mission. Their work focuses on four powerful universal archetypes: Lover, Warrior, Magician, and King. They support men to nurture the growth and development of each of these aspects so they are accessible when they are needed. Although their work is designed for men, the energetics of each archetype is crucial for women, too, as we innately seek to be reunited with these internal powers. The Lover has the soul fire to burn through all obstacles to love, internally and externally. It's the part of you that also knows how to hold yourself in love. The Warrior takes a stand for what you believe in and is unafraid to act and to change. The Magician sees the possibilities and potentials, both in people and situations. It asks, "What would you like to attract to you? I will help you bring it to fruition." The King is your discerning inner knowing, regal in stature. It knows when you are being your best self. The King understands that we are spiritual beings, connected to all that is.

Identifying aspects of self as "masculine" and "feminine" was essential to me in my soul inquiry as I went through my journey, and it's been helpful when I talk to other people, as well. To be clear, the point here is not to pigeonhole and confine us to traditional gender roles. We can, in fact, learn not to define ourselves by our gender and the traditional roles of what it means to be masculine like a sword and feminine as a flower. But if you are experiencing the loss of a love, thinking in terms of "masculine" and "feminine" helps highlight one of the hardest aspects of dealing with this kind of loss: that in your life together with someone, you create separate roles for each of you, and then when you are no longer in that life together, those roles fall apart and you must do and take on everything.

In your relationship, who was responsible for balancing the

checkbook and paying the bills? Who took out the garbage and changed the lightbulbs? Who did the taxes and managed the retirement account? Who spent more time caring for the children in the day-to-day? Who watered the houseplants and who mowed the lawn? It doesn't matter who did what, but it matters that you face the reality of playing roles that your partner played in the past—while practicing those aspects of what it means to be feminine or masculine in ordinary life.

This can affect women and men equally. Amyr came to me through Richard's books and his work in psychology, and I realized he was a candidate for my What Now? mentorship group, even though he was among women. He and his wife had decided that it would be in their best financial interests if she accepted a position in upper management and they relocated to Europe for what would likely be at least three years. They had two elementary-school-aged children, so Amyr decided that he would be a stay-at-home dad for this time period. A bright man with much potential, he didn't realize just how emasculating this period of separation from his career and role as a provider would become to his identity. He was feeling lost and confused about his identity, which had felt rock solid to him up until this point. The pain of this crisis was Amyr's initiation. He suffered depression and only felt good while he was running his daily ten-mile loop. So during this unique chapter of his life, I began to speak to Amyr about the inherent opportunities for him spiritually and how he could develop his more nurturing qualities and integrate the feminine into his being. I also encouraged him to see this time as a precious gift and opportunity to explore all of his potential passions and interests. I assured him there was plenty of time for him to return to his previously more structured work life and urged him to see this as a unique time to explore.

For some, like my good friends Bruce and Cindy, stepping into new roles and ways of being was the solution to the crisis rather than its spark. Over the years, I watched them as their journey of marriage and partnership unfolded. Bruce had been a successful executive business consultant, while Cindy dabbled in her own career passions in broadcasting. After a life-altering experience that included a potentially fatal cancer diagnosis, Bruce realized that his deepest desire was to live differently, and it seemed that for a time he passed the baton of earning and providing to Cindy. At this point, it became her responsibility to the family to bring in the income, and he became more homebound—managing the house and kids and other family business decisions. Over the years, I watched this man who was extremely masculine in the traditional ways, and who was built like a handsome hulk, become more of the nurturer, and not at a sacrifice to his masculine body builder's energy or physique. His choice to reverse roles with his wife did not diminish his masculine essence but rather completed him and allowed his sensitive and caring nature to flourish as he spent more time with his growing daughter. Cindy, on the other hand, entered the world of real estate during the post-2008 economic world crisis that also flourished. I saw how she used her femininity in a world dominated by male energy, making it an advantage, as Bruce held her space and helped her from the sidelines. At the same time, I watched as she began to integrate those same masculine qualities that I was learning about in managing Richard's position as a global brand leader. We were both discovering our ability to take action with discernment and decisiveness. We were polishing our ability to bring structure and order to our businesses and lives—all capacities of the masculine. Neither Cindy nor I have lost our feminine nature in the process, so well developed by having such masculine partners for so many years.

Cindy and Bruce have mastered the art of allowing each other to be both masculine and feminine equally. I believe that when each of us balances our energies we become the best version of ourselves, and I have surely witnessed the growth and success of this couple. Now they work together in different capacities in a thriving business that is held by both of them. Bruce owns his King and is a Warrior with heart, while Cindy is a sovereign Queen. Both have evolved into their greatest selves and live a life most look on with admiration, and possibly even envy. I look on having witnessed a couple grow in their commitment to holding space for each other to flourish, to become consciously whole in a sacred contract that is their destiny.

As is usually the case with crisis, Bruce's moment of initiation had a ripple effect on their lives. They surrendered and opened to life as it bid them to change. It required them to be deeply honest about what they both wanted to do and be next. Becoming their fuller, multidimensional selves, Cindy and Bruce were able to love each other more fully as well. And that is what this entire journey to wholeness prepares us to do: to love again, to love fully.

I recently interviewed Tom Zuba for my podcast. A noted life coach and author of the book *Permission to Mourn: A New Way to Do Grief*, Tom has endured great loss but is one of the most alive people I've ever met. He is supercharged with light and love. One might ask how he could lose so much: his young daughter, then his wife a few short years later to a rare blood disease, and then one son to cancer. Surviving all of that, he became a single father with one son, together becoming their own small family unit. He dove in deep and came out each time—likely wondering how and why he was chosen for *this*, but he grieved and healed, grieved and healed, and grieved and healed again. I know he's walked the hero's path many times, and it's been a rocky road indeed. Yet he is so alive and full of life after great loss, and he shares his ways of healing through grief with so many. He says, "Raising my sons without my wife allowed me to become both mother and father." He was able to integrate the feminine and masculine energies, also emerging whole as a result. As I do, he considers this among the gifts of his loss.

The love of the sovereign and whole self knows no bounds. Old habits of self-protection, shame, and unworthiness are transmuted into light by the power of its love. As we become reunited with the gifts of the masculine and feminine attributes and rooted in our sacred wholeness, we cannot help but love. There is no stopping that river.

SOVEREIGN UNFOLDING INTO WHOLENESS

At this point, above all, you have made the choice to fully embody being sovereign, which draws on all the heroic choices you have made along the way, and is also the last hero's choice.

What does this mean?

As a sovereign being, you are whole and completely self-governing. You are ready to serve and pursue your passion. Love is present to support you, but mastering the art of self-love and self-discovery is paramount to return to the joy of wholeness.

I have known many sovereign women and some men—some living on their own and some married. Each of them exudes a quality of true self-confidence that comes from self-love and self-respect. The sovereign woman or man regards collaboration and partnership as a fine companion but no substitute for his or her own opinions and values. The sovereign holds integrity like a sword. The sovereign is tuned-in to the body with complete awareness of physical and emotional needs. The sovereign appreciates structure and is fully integrated with a fine masculine sense of logic when solving problems but does not disregard the feminine principles of chaos, flow, and receptivity as the strongest of creative forces. The sovereign being is not rigid but remains malleable, like clay, yet walks with sure footing and makes choices from clear-minded thinking. The sovereign values what is sustainable. The sovereign relishes the clarity in stillness and the ability to surrender personal will for the higher will of the divine, opening the heart to the call of spirit. The sovereign encapsulates the Great Mother but also has the skills of the intentional archer, Artemis, and targets goals with effective accuracy, commitment, and action. The sovereign being is independent and discerning. Sovereigns have their own unique style and are completely comfortable with who they are as individuals. Being sovereign means feeling worthy of abundance. Most of all, the sovereign is aware and fully present and knows they are enough as they are.

YOU WERE BORN TO LOVE . . .
AGAIN AND AGAIN

At this point in your healing journey, are you still afraid to open to love again? Afraid to dive in? Understandable. But what if underneath the storm of heartbreak you have weathered and beneath all the blocks to love that the ego has formed around your heart, there is a world of love and feelings of joy that are completely perfect, like a well-guarded egg that you've been sitting on just waiting to burst out and to be seen?

There is nothing wrong with you.

In fact, there's nothing to do to be who you are. That statement seems so contradictory to the self-improvement era, doesn't it? You've been given so many lists of what you need to know, how you need to speak, what you need to do to be this or that or attract him or her. Truth is, contrary to the world of self-improvement, you don't create yourself at all; you reveal yourself. Layer by layer, as you heal, each block is removed and shows more. That's what emerging into wholeness is. Your time has come to be who you are without censoring and altering what you allow people to see versus what is. There is no difference—no app is needed to create a filter or change your image in order for you to be loved and fully embraced, to love and accept who you are. It is *you* that is hidden under those blocks that have been placed there for protection by your small-minded ego. As the hero and heroine, it is up to you to now confront the question of exactly what you are being protected from.

I know you're saying, "That's an easy answer—from the heartbreak I have suffered!"

I understand. But you can't feel this way forever. That strategy hasn't really worked well, has it? You weren't protected—that was an illusion—and you won't be again. And you need no protection. You are born to love and be loved and fully express who you are. There is no place to hide from love. I know it sounds like mumbo-jumbo and trite, but it's true—*it really is*. You are love, but fear of not being accepted and of possibly being abandoned blocks you from allowing your love to be present, given, and shared. It keeps you from feeling fully whole. As you change this and dare to love again, love is returned to you as you return to give more love.

It's easy to make the reason why our relationships don't work personal and about us. *Why didn't he call me back after that first date? What's wrong with me? How come he didn't text me after we hooked up?* Our negative self-talk—which begins with self-critical thoughts measuring if we are "good enough" or personalizing what we think someone else thinks about us—is the first block to remove. It's not about you—it's about them and their blocks to love. You are the one reading this book. You care more than most and have the wisdom to question and contemplate, and the bravery to remove your blocks to love despite the fact that by doing so you may suffer loss again.

I doubt, however, you will ever suffer the same. That's how wisdom works. As you evolve and emerge whole, connected to spirit, you aren't the same and won't ever feel the way you did again. You may never feel as vulnerable as you do now, either, because the wisdom and strength you have gained will not armor you but allow you to embrace and hold more feeling as you hold truth. You will be stronger this time.

After being hurt so many times, it would be easy to just give up on love. Certainly, as I am now exploring dating in the adult world, I am realizing that there are many people who do give up on love. What they don't realize is that they will only receive from giving. Love is an endless figure eight, but it is only one circle without connection if the person is shut off and purely focused on the physical body and not present with heart. It is our open heart that allows us to vibrate and offer more to another—more to all. This is now confirmed by science. The acclaimed research of educator Stephen G. Post, author of *Why Good Things Happen to Good People*, confirms that when we contribute to one another and give wholeheartedly, we are happier, healthier, and more successful human beings.

It's easy to get busy and tell yourself, *I don't need a relationship.* And certainly this is the time to explore an adventure of your soul without being tied down. However, one block to love to become aware of is that some people hide in their busyness—shielded by their overflowing Google calendar. They shut themselves off from love by a routine of too much activity. I can do this by immersing myself in my work and family life—creating a busy schedule, moving so much, traveling, not staying in one place long enough to spend quality time building real connections. I see many other people doing this, too.

Addiction blocks love. All forms of it. Sex, drugs, and alcohol. All are used to numb and stop the feelings that are too painful.

Ultimately, all of these suffice momentarily to stop the feelings of suffering but build a wall around the ability to be seen as you are—in all of your sober glory.

Life is short. If love is present at the door, open your arms to it and hold it tightly, because in time, we are all asked to let go lightly. There's no time like the present to love unabashedly—you are worthy to experience love again. Time and time again, no matter your age. If you ask widows and widowers if they would trade the heartbreak of loss for not having experienced the love they shared—I've never met one that would say so. Whether divorced or widowed, it is better to love—and lose—than not to experience a love that alters you forever. You may have had your heart broken, but love's wind will carry you a long way if you allow yourself to be swept up in it again and again.

It is an egoless path to dive into love and to dare to meet another person, soul to soul. While ego can make a convincing case for not risking love—understandably, because it doesn't want to be fired from its post of keeping you under a rock and "safe" at all costs—ego cannot exist in the presence of love that is unconditional and heart-centered.

Richard taught me how to love unconditionally because that's what he did. I was loved and embraced fully from the time I was eighteen to forty-three. I can't remember him ever criticizing me once. He would gently prod me in a direction when I needed guidance, but it was with tremendous kindness. He was never cross with me, nor I with him. We fully embraced love in the most healthy way, and that's what I learned how to do and give—whether it be to my children, my friends, or a lover. I practiced how to love without expectation as I mirrored a master.

Each of us can reflect on our past loves and what was learned in the connection—being thankful for that growth. Looking for what you've gained amidst your loss will free you from the shackles of suffering. And, my friend, you have gained your freedom, above all. You are free to have your love affair with life. Engage fully in all of it because it is yours to do so.

I know of a woman who recently met "the perfect man." Divorced for the third time, she has spent the past year dating and enjoying her freedom while also making a strong connection to the divine after a year of suffering and healing. In this chance meeting with this man, she dove all in, heart and soul, for a few months, only to find that even though he seemed the perfect match for her—some magic was missing. And she began to realize that the magic she felt on her own surpassed what she felt while sharing life with someone who wasn't feeling 100 percent right for her. She has learned to follow her heart and listen to her passion. She is navigating her life differently now from this place of wholeness she feels. She is making choices and decisions from the vantage point of her sovereign self.

NEVER GIVE UP

Finding freedom and joy after a long passage of suffering sometimes seems unimaginable. Mario Scharmer and his brother, Miguel, had grown up next door, and our families were close. His mom, Chris, was also a Sai Baba devotee, and we shared much along the spiritual path together. Years earlier, when we had bought the house next door to her, it had been the answer to her prayer of desiring to live in a like-minded community of people who shared many of her spiritual interests and values. Her youngest son, Mario, grew up to be an attractive, charismatic, popular young man. When Mario was eighteen years old, his life took an abrupt turn. One predawn morning after some heavy partying, he drove his car into a traffic pole that sliced the car in half. He was dead on arrival at the hospital for six minutes before they revived him, and his mom received the 3:00 A.M. call that shattered their lives. Yet he lived. For several months, Mario lay limp in an induced coma due to head trauma and brain damage.

I began to see the heroine's journey of a fiercely courageous and loving mother emerge right from the start as Chris refused to believe the doctors who told her that her son would be a brain-dead vegetable. She spent hours in the hospital room for many months listening to all the beeps and buzzes of the monitors, and after a while she began to realize that Mario was communicating with her through his heart-rate monitor. As he became agitated his heart rate would speed up, and as he became calm and happier it would slow down. Long after the staff had said the heart-rate monitor was no longer needed, Chris insisted that it stay right where it was. Having been a teacher of youngsters (kindergarten through third grade), and having done extensive research on the brain, Chris knew that even though Mario seemed inactive, he likely was still experiencing stimuli. This motivated her to create a small file box containing a schedule of activities for energizing his sensory perception. The box was labeled with the categories it included inside: touch, smell, feeling, hearing, sight. She enlisted volunteers—family and friends—to spend at least half an hour once per week with Mario, using feathers, essential oils, music, reading, and a number of other healing tools to stimulate his brain and begin to get his synapses firing and neuro-pathways reestablished. The miracle of a mother's love started to show as Mario opened his eyes. Clearly he was far more than the doctors believed he would ever be. And he obviously understood what had happened to him, although he could not communicate or move much. His eyes told a different story, one that said, "I know what I did. I know where I am."

Now, as you can imagine, this has not been a journey for the meek or weary. Trying to convince an eighteen-year-old boy that his life still has meaning and to give him the faith and courage to continue was one of the greatest challenges. Chris and her husband, Mark, Mario's adoptive father, have been devoted beyond the imaginable to his recovery. And Mario has had his moments of facing the greatest dragon, which ushered him and his parents deep into the valley of despair, where surrender to the divine became the inevitable choice.

One night, long after Chris had brought him home from a facility that was not caring for him properly, Mario lay in his hospital bed in the living room. He was incredibly frustrated at being a full-care patient, unable to move from his bed and unable to talk. Chris was doing their evening ritual of care when Mario bit her hand to the bone as she was putting his feeding tube in. He had been fighting her for days, and she grew weary and finally retreated to her own room in tears. She knew he was telling her he didn't want to do this life any longer. As Chris lay in her bed in complete surrender, a miracle was under way. Mario slept for three days, and when he awoke, he did so with a beaming white-light smile. He had also surrendered and woke up in love with life.

Mario went from wishing to die to full acceptance of this new life, a very different life than he had planned. After many healing modalities, and much tenacity, struggle and hard work, today he lives on his own, walks with a walker, and does his best to mouth words. His speech is limited, but his brain functions well. While he doesn't live the life he would have, he is a miracle of love. He is an extremely talented artist with an expressed mission to spread love to the world through his art and offer his loving presence.

Together, this family, refusing to accept the news they were given, embarked on a journey of "raising Mario twice," which is the title of the book Chris wrote about their story. They have all chosen the hero's path, and they've arrived into wholeness and have returned to joy, accepting their new circumstances, facing adversity with courage and faith, surrendering to the divine, and, most important, loving so purely despite the extreme challenges they have faced over the years.

Chris has said to me, "I've come to realize that in healing Mario, I've healed myself. I live in far less fear today than I ever did. And I love my life even though it hasn't been at all easy."

When you love life more than any one horrifying tragedy that happens, eventually you return to your love of life, and that's what sustains you and gives you the hope, faith, and courage to continue on. To live more. To love more. To live bigger. To return to joy.

FROM GRIEF TO GRATITUDE—
THE FLOWERING OF JOY

One of the hallmarks of wholeness is coming to a place of contentment and peace within, where you feel completely aligned and in tune with who you are now. You have come through the corridor of loss and into a vibrant, abundant expression that is anchored in strength, wisdom, and gratitude. You have integrated your lessons of the archetypal feminine and masculine energies, and you know you are completely responsible for your own life.

You are now ready to return to joy.

HeartMath, an institute credited for the research scientifically proving the great emotional intelligence of the heart, says, "Joy is the expression of gratitude in the heart." Returning from grief to gratitude is a mile marker that lets you know you are well on your way to being whole.

In his much-loved book *The Prophet*, Kahlil Gibran says, "Your joy is your sorrow unmasked." These six words spoke to me and whispered hope in my ear as I weathered the storm of grief that came after Richard's transition. I died a death when he did. And I began my journey of mending a broken heart that was filled with sorrow—sorrow that leaked through the cracks of a shattered life, while spilling out the tears of a thousand years.

About three months after Richard's memorial, I attended a book-launch party for a dear friend, Mike Robbins, and his first book, *Focus on the Good Stuff.* Richard had finished the foreword to it just three weeks before he died. I felt obligated to attend the party on Richard's behalf. As happy as I wanted to feel for our friend, I was hardly ready to celebrate anything that resembled my previous life that had all too fleetingly been pulled right out from under my feet. It felt more like a public assault when people who knew me and knew our story looked my way. I'm sure it was only because I felt naked and raw that I felt so exposed to their gaze.

People mean well when they say things to you, but often hearing no words is better comfort to someone grief-stricken than hearing the wrong words.

A man approached me and said, "You know, you are very lucky to have lived such a great love with Richard in your lifetime. You should be very grateful."

I stared in blank disbelief as if he had slapped my face. Then he proceeded with the usual and awkward "I'm sorry for your loss."

My response: "What do you mean? Loss? I didn't lose my car keys. My life was annihilated. I'm sorry, but I don't feel grateful. I feel devastated."

I walked away and found a post to lean on outside on a stairway in the fresh air.

As soon as he said the word "grateful," I knew I felt anything but gratitude for the pain I was experiencing, and I resented him for saying that I should. I wasn't sure I would ever feel grateful for having the kind of love that was so painful to lose.

In time, I changed. And so did my attitude.

I don't consider that the acceptance of my loss was the ending point to grief, but rather the portal to living more life. When I accepted my loss, I began to embrace and step into a new life—one walking solo but not alone.

That's when I decided midlife is not a crisis unless you are in one. It is a time of inquiry: *Who am I now?*

Years later, it's been quite a remarkable journey of self-discovery, with lots of twists and turns, and blessings, too. Now I've returned to a deep feeling of gratitude for having loved so honestly, purely, and with true and lasting fulfillment. People ask me if I'll remarry, and my response is, "I don't know." My cup is more than half-filled with enough love from Richard to potentially last my lifetime.

I do know that I find myself in prayer a lot of the time at this point in my journey. As I close my eyes at night and open them in the morning, my mind is speaking my prayers of thanksgiving. I am so grateful for all that life is and the abundance and joy of this experience. My prayers are different now. Rather than communicating with a God outside myself, I feel directly connected to a supreme presence. And to that presence my prayers are always prayers of thanks— prayers that come from the joy of being alive.

I am truly grateful for having loved so deeply that I know now I am better for it. I would do it all over again with the same soul contract in place because loving Richard and being loved by him were indeed worth the heartbreak—worth the loss and every tear.

Gratitude and noticing the many things in your life that you're thankful for, both past and present, can be a great salve for a broken heart. Now that you have gone through the processes of inquiry and healing leading up to this final chapter of the book, I would like to invite you to write a gratitude letter. This is a love letter of thanks that you can now write with your whole heart. Whom or what would you like to express your feelings of soul-level appreciation for?

For a little extra inspiration to get you started, the following gratitude letter is one that I wrote to Richard ten years after he left this earth.

My Dearest Richard,

December 13th . . . I am in awe that it's been ten years on this journey without you.

I mean, not really without you, because I carry you—or, you carry me—every day. I often feel you walking beside me, or next to me as I'm writing. I sense your presence from your side of our bed.

The one thing I realized very early on is that our love connects us. We are but two sparks of the same flame. I've understood that death is only separation from human form. It is our love that continues beyond.

Even so, it has been a journey, and somehow this tenth anniversary marks a feeling of completion for me. When you first transitioned, I felt so incomplete—so shattered. Our perfect world had crumbled and the rug was pulled out from under us. It took a long time for me to find the floor. But once I did, my feet started running.

I don't miss you any less, but I have learned to live my life without your physical presence. I still miss you, my love, and often close my eyes or slip into a reverie where I call in that old familiar feeling of safety that you gave me. I could always land with you in a nest of unconditional love.

In my lows, I call on you to assist me and guide me in what to do. I know what you would say and how you would think in a situation. You are pure light now, and you infuse me every day.

We were great together, and I learned so much from you about how to live a happy life. The beauty is, our relationship continues on.

The lessons and gifts I've received over the years through this journey of healing and growth have shown me how to be strong and step into all things with courage. I've truly learned how to lean into my greatest fears—and not too much scares me anymore.

I've always remembered the early message in the mess that came from your words: "Your circumstances don't make or break you, but rather, reveal who you are. And the beauty of the human spirit is we can take our greatest tragedy and allow it to move us forward, adding greater meaning to our lives." These words elevated me from the trenches of despair and out of the tragedy of our story.

I'm not sure what my life would be like with you at my side, in form—probably stable and surefooted—not so craggy a road with as many twists and turns with opportunists who were villains along the way. But I have leaned into those lessons, too, as discernment was critical for me to learn. You held my space to become a truly feminine woman, and now I've had to integrate the masculine qualities, too.

I am feeling whole and complete in ways I never imagined. I am strong, competent, and confident with deep wisdom that has been well earned by my intense life experience. I am a sovereign woman now. My life has unfolded—not without its share of drama—but I have arrived safely from all of my initiations and the situations that arose with chaos.

I am so grateful for all that you gave me in our lives together in love, and I am so grateful for this journey of healing, as well.

You have been my master teacher, my love. You are my twin flame and I always feel you fanning the fire within me—to carry on.

We are celebrating twenty years of Don't Sweat the Small Stuff this year . . . Can you even believe that? Twenty years—25 million books—well over 100 million readers. That's crazy!

I can feel you jumping with joy! You loved your work, and your work lives on. Your words still touch millions of lives and will continue to comfort and reassure people that all will be well, and life isn't so scary.

We have three grandchildren and a fourth on the way. Oh, how I wish you could have held them and played with them. It is such a joy, and I love being a Nana! Someday, they will read your books and know you, too. Caden, the oldest, now seven, recently saved your photo to his desktop on his iPad. It melted my heart to see your happy face smiling back at him.

Life isn't all rainbows and butterflies—I know that now. But the things I am now certain of are:

Change is hard but necessary. Growth means maximizing our human potential even amidst adversity. Being present is the key. Gratitude is what it means to live in joy. And most importantly . . .

Love never dies.

Love transcends the boundaries of time and space.

Love lasts forever; indeed, it does.

I will always celebrate your life. I will always honor you with mine.

Thank you with all my heart for the gifts of you. Thank you for sharing your life with me.

I love you,

Kris

My Gratitude Letter

Dear _____,

I am grateful for

_____

_____

_____

_____

_____.

Thank you for

_____

_____

_____

_____.

With all my love,

xo

Yes, your heart will be broken open to more than you can possibly imagine. But remember that the depth that you feel your sorrow is the depth that you will feel your joy. And when you can focus on what love has brought to you—the gifts it has brought to you—more than what you've lost, that's when you know that you're on your hero's journey to wholeness.

ARE YOU READY FOR MORE?

The biggest question is: Are you now ready for more? More love. More adventure. More romance. More to share. More story. More meaning. More life!

Not long ago, a friend asked why I have not remarried. Part of my soul contract has been to heal those wounded parts of myself that were afraid of being alone; those masculine parts that I had deferred to Richard had remained incomplete in the shadow of my marriage and partnership with a very strong man. In my case, the gift has been the deep joy and bliss of meeting my fears and moving through the messy process of transformation. I've come through the hoop of fire and out the other side in ways that have brought me such feelings of peace and joy, and have taught me what it means to feel whole and no longer broken. I've learned and grown so much I can't even recognize myself from those younger years. (Except I still have my enthusiasm and bubbly nature—I love to laugh!)

Over the years, I have dated and been in relationships and have also gone through periods of celibacy. My sexual needs and desires don't drive me as hard as they did in my forties. Now, in my fifties, much of my sexual energy that in my younger years was driven by raging hormones manifests in my creativity and my work for greater productivity—for the most part, anyway. I'm reminded of a gay couple I met on a plane last year on my way to Montreal, Canada. They were both in their seventies and had only been together as a couple for one year. They talked to me about how they were totally in love and traveling the world together, and how before they met neither of them thought that they would ever experience passionate, intimate love again. One of them looked me in the eyes with such a depth of self-understanding, saying, "We still have the desire to be physical with each other, but then we realize that we're just too tired!" We all let out a big belly laugh at the sweet honesty of this statement.

The very best part of where I am now is the deep well of peace I feel inside. I no longer worry about being alone—or whether another life partner will show up. I surrender and trust in the divine completely. I know the universe has my back. I am open to meeting someone who wants to share the wonderlust I feel for more of all the good stuff love has to offer. I would love a playmate who is also a soul mate who has arrived along the journey into wholeness himself. When one complete person meets another and there is a strong chemistry, then you can embark on a journey to enjoy the fruits of life together, where you walk as two sovereign beings in love. I know several married couples that have made it this far and into thirty years. My own parents have been married fifty-seven years with barely a hiccup. This is what I hope for, but it's not a longing. As I've said, my love cup will always remain half full from the life I shared with Richard. So many of my fears have evaporated with the expression of so much life. Like you, I've lived an incredibly rich life already. I'm especially grateful for my daughters, my son-in-law, and my grandchildren. (I now have four—yes, *four*—grandkids. And I'm Nana! Not Grandma!) I feel blessed that both my parents are alive and healthy. The other half is my adventure now, and one I will navigate from a place of wholeness and joy—following all that makes me feel excited and alive.

I have loved deeply. I've lost and grieved greatly. I've traveled the long road home—from grief to gratitude. And yes, I can now say with a healed heart that it truly is better to have loved deeply and lost than to never have loved that way at all. That love, like so many other amazing memories, is imprinted on my soul to push me forward into the next chapter.

Most important, I've found my way back to the joy that comes from having a love affair with life itself. A love affair with life doesn't mean having to be alone; however, it does mean having a wonderlust experience, where your lust for more drives you and excitement is what ignites you. You get to wake up every day and say, "Wow, I get another one of these!" Your love of life and spirit; your love of family, friends, and community; your work; the earth—they all become a wheel of passion, and you cannot separate or settle for anything less than what that lust for more aliveness drives you to: living completely in joy and awake. Even while you are traveling the long road of healing your sorrow, you can choose joy. Laughter and joy are present every day, and you can open to them and allow them to carry you without guilt.

CHOOSING YOURSELF, COMMITTING TO LIFE

Certain people are obviously born to be leaders, and you can spot them very young. They are lemonade-stand entrepreneurs, star athletes, environmental and social activists, valedictorians, and class presidents. But most of us must come into our power and learn the art of leadership as we grow up, with some of us being late bloomers. No matter when we come to claim it, we are all students of life and leaders of love.

Over the phases of our lives from childhood into adolescence and into our adult and senior years, we can track these periods as being maidens and apprentice warriors, parents and providers, and finally wise women and men. Each of these time periods should and could have its own ritual rites of passage.

Many cultures do have rites of passage from one stage of life to the next. These very special transitions and progressions seem to have been lost to many Western cultures, and this leaves us dangling with unfinished business in areas of our lives that would be better served by seeing an ending and a step into a new time, giving us more confidence and the joy of feeling supported by our community.

Now you can create your own ritual rite of passage into your sovereignty, marking a new time in your life—a symbolic marriage-vow ceremony. This is a life-changing ritual that my friend Christine Arylo introduced me to. Christine is the author of *Choosing Me Before We.* This book is a must-read for those who have come out of a long-term relationship for whatever reason and for those who have lost their identity to that relationship.

One summer evening, Christine came over to do a ceremony with me of choosing myself to love first. There was a glorious sunset with a cool breeze blowing, and I was wearing an ivory dress adorned with lace, long seashell earrings, and a shell necklace—a sconce of evolution. We lit candles, and I read my vows, declaring and affirming my new commitment to love myself and to be in love with life above all. This was my first commitment to being sovereign.

As you feel ready to make this commitment to yourself, I invite you to prepare for it with the utmost care, being thoughtful of giving your word and how you would like it to affect the days of your life. How can this rite of passage bring you closer to yourself, where you come to know yourself even more intimately? How can it inspire you to care for your life with greater consistency and always in step with your highest values? Just as many marriage ceremonies are preceded by a period of spiritual counseling and contemplation, I recommend taking a thirty-day period to work with the following points of **preparation** (internal focus) and **planning** (external focus):

PREPARATIONS FOR YOUR CEREMONY

1. **Ignite your passion and purpose to create a life of meaning.**
   Rediscovering what truly makes your heart sing is what it

means to feel passion. Follow what excites you and it will ignite you. Sometimes we have to look back to the past and remember those "heart sing" things that we might have left behind in order to live a "responsible" life or an "efficient" life. What lights you up, smiling ear to ear? What would you do if you had no barriers of time or money or circumstance standing in your way? Remember, just behind your passion is your purpose, and knowing your purpose is one of the great joys of life.

2. **Know what your fun factor is.** When you think of having fun, what are you doing? Do *more* of that! Do you like to hike, dine out, travel, do yoga, mountain bike, write poetry? Make a list, and make it a point to do at least three of these things that are your fun factors each week. Schedule time on your calendar for them, and then keep the appointment. (For couples: date night is a *must*!!) Whatever it is that means fun to you, make sure you are blocking out time daily and weekly to do those things that add pleasure to your life. Pleasure is as important as doing work that you love; sometimes, if you're as lucky as I am, those are one and the same.

3. **Be mindfully engaged in your life.** As you become more mindful in your everyday life, engaged in your activities and relationships while increasing your fun and rediscovering what lights you up, your life will feel richer and more meaningful. Practice noticing the sky and feeling the quality of the air on your skin. Go on a walk and notice all that's surrounding your path and how it feels to place your feet one in front of the other. Make a practice of breathing deeply and feeling what's happening in your body and in your heart. Whenever you might feel like something is missing, see if what is missing is *you*.

4. **Discover your sovereign choices.** Not all choices are created equal; some leave you feeling more connected to yourself and have far-reaching impact on your life as a whole. Every time you take supreme care of yourself, as you began to do in chapter 2, you are simultaneously exercising supreme discipline as you hold the integrity of your commitments to yourself and others. Be a true "yes" when something feels right to you, and a true "no, thank you" when it feels wrong. When you realize your one great love—your love of life—either something adds to it or takes from it. Your sovereign choices are those that always add to and enrich your life.

5. **Be open to divine guidance.** You deserve heaven's help, and it's always available to you. Holding you in every single moment, even those where you feel wholly alone, is a divine presence. Practice watching for, listening for, and feeling into its signs and signals. The more you do so, the more quickly you will amplify this constant conversation you are having with Life.

PLANNING FOR YOUR CEREMONY

- *What is your time frame? In your calendar, write down the month, day, and time of your ceremony.*
- *What will you wear to this auspicious occasion?*
- *Will you have a ring? Or will you choose another symbol as a reminder of your commitment?*
- *Who would you like to have witness your ceremony and support your commitment?*
- *Where would you like to have it? At the sea, in the forest, at home?*

In the sacred walk home to your Self, the following vows represent the promise to love in a way that will carry you through all of the ups and downs of this wild and beautiful roller-coaster life of yours. They are offered here as inspiration for you. Change or add to them as you are guided to.

The Sovereign Commitment Ceremony
Your Promise to Self and Life

From this day forward I will love life first.

*Having a love affair with my life means I will follow my joy.
It means I will engage freely and untethered to thoughts of fear
that I am not worthy of such a love affair.*

*This is my one precious life, and I plan to live it as a wild
adventure—fully aware that I am navigating my own ship,
fully embracing this experience of soul learning.*

*I will continue to dive deep for the wisdom that is mine through my
soul inquiry: those questions I ask to retrieve the wisdom I need to
move forward on the path of love.*

*This is my commitment to love my life first, before anything else.
As I love this life—I am grateful for this new beginning.*

*Loving life is loving the mirror of me in my life. All things show up
for me. All things show up to teach me something and reveal me to
myself. I am one with all that is present.*

*To the supreme presence that surrounds me: I'm ready to be your
instrument and to be ever more intuitively alive; to step into life
with fresh eyes and a new perspective. I will be divinely guided and
inspired for the rest of my days.*

*I am forever committed to my divine purpose of being an
instrument of light and love.*

I am one in my own precious life.

I love my life.

———

I was speaking at Christina Rasmussen's first live Life Starters event in November of 2013 when a very kind woman walked up to me. I remember feeling such compassion for her as she told me her husband had been riding his bike home from work and was hit by a car and killed. The young man who was driving was in his twenties. He had been texting while driving and didn't even know that he'd killed him. I remember her asking, "Can you tell me how long this takes? This is just so painful." Judith Finneren was in the phase of grief where it feels like death, but she took her tragedy and created a monument to her husband—"the ghost bike"—that has turned into a movement and also an award-winning documentary film. It has been about four years since I met Judith, and she has found new love while embarking on a whole new career. Her return to joy happened earlier for her than some because she has found her way to live and to move forward carrying her late husband with her. She is one of my heroes—just like Lisa, Christina Rasmussen, Carolyn Moor, Mario and Chris, Tom Zuba, and all the others I've mentioned in this book. All were ordinary people at some time, but all have allowed their tragedy, their heartbreak and loss, to drive them forward to create a life of extraordinary meaning. They are all heroes and heroines sharing a message that comes through a story of how the human spirit triumphs over tears and tragedy. This is the choice we all have in front of us. How you choose to heal determines the course you will walk. You, too, can be the hero of your own story. You, too, can step into real and lasting joy. You, too, can serve humanity by choosing to be the hero you are born to be.

SOUL MANTRA:

Stand with your eyes open while looking in a mirror,
arms stretched out as far as you can reach and legs
open in a triangle. As you breathe in love to every cell,
exhale fear. Repeat until you feel it in your bones and
it resonates in your heart:

I am whole now. I am home. I am. I am. I am.

THE SOUL INQUIRY:
I AM WHOLE AND SOVEREIGN

Please retrieve your journal and answer these questions:

1. What have I learned from my experience and loss?
2. Am I feeling more comfortable in my own skin?
3. In what ways am I feeling whole and complete?
4. What is my inner voice whispering to me at this point? Is anything within me needing my attention, compassion, and love right now?
5. What advice would I give someone in heartbreak now?
6. Am I ready to share my story now?
7. If so, how will I share my story? (with one person or many)

Your New Story • *transformational writing process*

Your return to joy. Write about your new love affair with life. From this place of wholeness and completion, what will your life look like moving forward? How will you express your aliveness, and how will that support you when life's challenges and losses come? How will you choose to live your hero's journey from this day forward?

_____

_____

_____

_____

_____

_____

_____

A Word Before You Go . . .

This book has been a complete joy; I couldn't even stop it from birthing. It was as if the baby had already crowned—I could not stop it from coming. After writing *Don't Sweat the Small Stuff for Moms*, I needed to recover from the stalker and build my social media platforms and spend many years offering great content on my website to build an online following. I waited until I heard the divine call on this book. I was speaking to a dear friend one day who is a transformational leader himself, and he said, "I want the world to know the depth of your wisdom, Kris"—and in about half an hour we outlined a book. Over the next months, it's as if the divine opened all the doors for this book to come into form. *From Heartbreak to Wholeness* was birthed from love, just the way my children came into this world. This book is my gift to you, a heartbroken soldier, who has returned from the battle and now is ready to heal. I dedicated this book to a woman, Lisa, who has been a soul-mate friend—a sister to me. I was terrified the past year that I might lose another person I love. I watched in awe as Lisa met her journey with cancer with such courage, and she squeezed all the growth she could out of that cancer. She used it to awaken, and she walked her hero's path and is now cancer-free. We all endure, and we all have the same opportunity to learn, grow, and awaken to deeper meaning and greater joy. The divine gave me bread crumbs to follow for every chapter, and it was simply a joy to be here with you on this journey and in these pages.

I live by the notion that we are all students of life and leaders of love. It doesn't matter what you do as long as you do it with love. Whether it be in small acts of kindness or greater acts of legacy leadership, we lead by our example, and it is indeed as Gandhi said: Your life is your message. We can all choose to be the hero of our story and hence choose to love humanity by sharing what we've learned along the way. In large ways and through small deeds every day: We Live. We Love. We Let Go.

As I finish this book for you, my broken foot is almost completely healed. There is but a remnant of injury as I step in and back to my life. This broken foot mending these past eight weeks as I've been working on chapters of emerging, rebirthing, and returning to wholeness does not escape me as a great metaphor. I've had some messy days dealing with myself in this process of healing, as temporary as it was, feeling stuck and isolated. I've had to practice a new kind of mindfulness in my body—ever so attentive to my fragility. I had to rearrange my routine, and ask for help because I couldn't drive, and it's been a process of healing that is both emotional and physical. This served well to make me remember how it feels to have the disruption of loss and how we must adjust to embrace a healing time period. I have questioned: *Am I really and truly whole and complete with my journey?*

Then I remember that wholeness itself is a process and a journey, one you enter and reenter like walking the labyrinth, where you step into and out of the center many times before you reach the end. And what is an ending but a beginning?

You have conquered the unimaginable and unthinkable to emerge free to embrace the epic journey that is your life. It is your choice to choose the path of the one heart—to choose the hero's journey along the path of love. As you continue to embody wholeness, you will awaken to deeper meaning, deeper joy, and a new beginning.

The ultimate truth is that there is really no ending and no beginning—just one endless loop after loop in the infinite figure eight of life and love, where your connections to love never die.

I feel Richard every day—I feel his love.

Thank you for having the courage to do this work, to go through the soul inquiry, and to frame your story as the hero's journey. Mostly, I am honored that you are here to reveal who you are, and moreover, to remember why you are here as the hero you are: to share your message and offer your hand; to be the divinely guided and inspired instrument to humanity as you evolve and change and alchemize the world into peace, harmony, and a place where we can continue to be committed to love; to lust for more wonder; and to live in unapologetic wholeness and in joy.

You're the only one who can be you, and you are never alone, because as you love life, it loves you back. You are here to share the fullness of who you are and the timeless wisdom that comes through your process and your story. Humankind will change and evolve as you and I allow change to uncover our blocks to love. You are the hero of your story now. You are the hero you've been waiting for.

Treasure the gifts of life and love.
Treasure the journey.

Resources

RESOURCES BY KRISTINE CARLSON

Website
www.kristinecarlson.com

Books
From Heartbreak to Wholeness: The Hero's Journey to Joy, publication date June 12, 2018

Heartbroken Open: A Memoir Through Loss to Self-Discovery

An Hour to Live, an Hour to Love: The True Story of the Best Gift Ever Given

Don't Sweat the Small Stuff for Moms: Simple Ways to Stress Less and Enjoy Your Family More

Don't Sweat the Small Stuff for Women: Simple and Practical Ways to Do What Matters Most and Find Time for You

Don't Sweat the Small Stuff in Love: Simple Ways to Nurture and Strengthen Your Relationships

Retreats & Workshops
What Now?—Kristine's signature retreat includes three unforgettable days along the Northern California coast, plus a 6-week virtual course.

See her website for a complete schedule of retreats and other events.

BLOG: www.kristinecarlson.com/blog/
PODCAST: www.kristinecarlson.com/podcast/

OTHER FREE RESOURCES: http://kristinecarlson.com/resources/
30 Days of Don't Sweat Wisdom
The Power of Belief—eBook
Happiness Quote Images: Print, Desktop, and Lockscreen

Kristine Carlson on Social Media
FACEBOOK: www.facebook.com/KristineTeriCarlson
TWITTER: www.twitter.com/KristineCarlson
PINTEREST: www.pinterest.com/kriscarlsonbks
YOUTUBE: www.youtube.com/user/kristinecarlson2010

OTHER RESOURCES

Books
Achor, Shawn; *The Happiness Advantage: : The Seven Principles That Fuel Success and Performance at Work.*

Allen, David; *Getting Things Done: The Art of Stress-Free Productivity.*

Arylo, Christine; *Choosing Me Before We: Every Woman's Guide to Life and Love.*

Bailey, Joseph; *Slowing Down to the Speed of Life: How to Create a More Peaceful, Simpler Life from the Inside Out* (coauthored by Richard Carlson).

Bain, Barnet; *The Book of Doing and Being: Rediscovering Creativity in Life, Love, and Work.*

Bolen, Jean Shinoda; *Goddesses in Everywoman: Powerful Archetypes in Women's Lives.*

Campbell, Joseph; *The Hero with a Thousand Faces (The Collected Works of Joseph Campbell)* and *The Power of Myth.*

Carlson, Richard; *Don't Sweat the Small Stuff . . . and It's All Small Stuff: Simple Ways to Keep the Little Things from Taking Over Your Life* — and the entire *Don't Sweat the Small Stuff* series; *Easier Than You Think . . . Because Life Doesn't Have to Be So Hard;* and *You Can Be Happy No Matter What: Five Principles for Keeping Life in Perspective.*

DiPerna, Dustin; *Streams of Wisdom: An Advanced Guide to Integral Spiritual Development (Integral Religion and Spirituality Book 1)* (coauthored by Ken Wilber).

Gibran, Kahlil; *The Prophet.*

Hay, Louise; *Heal Your Body.*

Kübler-Ross, Elisabeth; *On Death and Dying: What the Dying Have to Teach Doctors, Nurses, Clergy and Their Own Families* and *On Grief and Grieving: Finding the Meaning of Grief Through the Five Stages of Loss.*

Murdock, Maureen; *The Heroine's Journey: Woman's Quest for Wholeness.*

Myss, Caroline; *Sacred Contracts: Awakening Your Divine Potential.*

Pausch, Randy; *The Last Lecture.*

Post, Stephen G.; *Why Good Things Happen to Good People: How to Live a Longer, Healthier, Happier Life by the Simple Act of Giving* (coauthored by Jill Neimark).

Rasmussen, Christina; *Second Firsts: Live, Laugh, and Love Again.*

Rendon, Jim; *Upside: The New Science of Post-Traumatic Growth*

Robbins, Mike; *Focus on the Good Stuff: The Power of Appreciation* and *Nothing Changes Until You Do: A Guide to Self-Compassion and Getting Out of Your Own Way.*

Salmansohn, Karen; *Think Happy: Instant Peptalks to Boost Positivity* and *Instant Happy Journal: 365 Days of Inspiration, Gratitude, and Joy.*

St. John-Dutra, Rich and Yvonne St. John-Dutra; *Be the Hero You've Been Waiting For.*

Scharmer, Christine (Chris); *Raising Mario Twice: How Love Can Transform a Life After a Tragic Event.*

Shapiro, Shauna; *The Art and Science of Mindfulness: Integrating Mindfulness Into Psychology and the Helping Professions* and *Mindful Discipline: A Loving Approach to Setting Limits and Raising an Emotionally Intelligent Child.*

Spilsbury, Ariel; *The 13 Moon Oracle: A Journey Through the Archetypal Faces of the Divine Feminine.*

Zuba, Tom; *Permission to Mourn: A New Way to do Grief.*

Teachers and Practitioners

Chödrön, Pema; American Buddhist teacher: www.pemachodronfoundation.org

Rasmussen, Christina: www.secondfirsts.com

Kornfield, Jack; American Buddhist teacher: www.jackkornfield.com

Shapiro, Shauna: www.drshaunashapiro.com

Wieder, Marcia; founder of Dream University: www.dreamuniversity.com

Transformational Organizations, Workshops, and Retreats

Challenge Day, founded by Rich Dutra-St. John and Yvonne St. John-Dutra: www.challengeday.org

The 52 Hike Challenge, founded by Karla Amador: www.52hikechallenge.com

HeartMath Institute: www.heartmath.org

Ghost Bike, founded by Judith Finneren: www.facebook.com/judith.finneren

The ManKind Project: www.mankindproject.org

The Modern Widows Club, founded by Carolyn Moor: modernwidowsclub.com

Path of Love retreats: www.pathretreats.com

Other

A Course in Miracles, Foundation for Inner Peace: www.acim.org

About the Author

Kristine Carlson is a *New York Times* bestselling author, speaker, and leader in the field of transformation. After collaborating with her late husband, Dr. Richard Carlson, to create a publishing industry phenomenon with the Don't Sweat the Small Stuff series—selling more than 25 million copies worldwide—Kris is emerging today as a profound teacher in the areas that matter most to the human heart: how to heal and how to love.

In addition to *From Heartbreak to Wholeness*, Kristine has captivated readers around the world with her previous books, which include *Don't Sweat the Small Stuff in Love; Don't Sweat the Small Stuff for Women; Don't Sweat the Small Stuff for Moms; An Hour to Live, an Hour to Love: The True Story of the Best Gift Ever Given;* and *Heartbroken Open: A Memoir Through Loss to Self-Discovery.*

Kristine offers her renowned retreats, workshops, and other live events internationally. As a sought-after speaker, she is known for her authenticity, vulnerability, and humor, leaving her audiences moved, inspired, and optimistic about the future. She has been featured on national radio and television, including *Today, Good Morning America, The View,* and *The Oprah Winfrey Show.*

Kristine has served on the board of directors and the Global Leadership Council for Challenge Day. She was honored to join the Go Red for Women campaign for the American Heart Association in

2012 as their keynote speaker. In 2010 she was honored with the Kennedy Laureate Award by John F. Kennedy University, an acknowledgment also given to Alice Waters and Dr. Sanjay Gupta for their work in the area of mental, physical, and spiritual well-being.

Kristine is Mom to two daughters and nana to four grandchildren. She lives in California.

PLEASE VISIT

....

FROMHEARTBREAKTOWHOLENESS.COM

....

TO RETRIEVE YOUR SOUL MANTRA
MEDITATION DOWNLOADS.